THE GREAT TEACHER OF JOURNALISTS

Fredonia Books
Amsterdam, The Netherlands

The Great Teacher of Journalists:
Kim Jong Il

ISBN: 1-4101-0124-X

Copyright © 2002 by Fredonia Books

Reprinted from the 1983 edition

Fredonia Books
Amsterdam, The Netherlands
http://www.fredoniabooks.com

All rights reserved, including the right to reproduce this book, or portions thereof, in any form.

The dear leader Comrade Kim Jong Il giving guidance on articles, pictures and layout for the *Rodong Sinmun*

The dear leader Comrade Kim Jong Il giving guidance to the work of Editorial Board of the *Rodong Sinmun*

The dear leader Comrade Kim Jong Il gives on-the-spot guidance to the Central News Agency

The dear leader Comrade Kim Jong Il examines the printed cakendar

PREFACE

Today, in Korea, the press is in its heyday, and journalists are giving full scope to their talent in their worthwhile activities, for the Party and the revolution.

New innovations and wonders which are being made every day in the press, the growing up of real men or genuine writers, and emotional legends of love for people are unthinkable apart from the wise guidance and utmost care of the dear Comrade Kim Jong Il, a great leader and a benevolent teacher.

He is always among journalists and teaches them every detailed problem arising in their activities, and kindly leads them to write and compile excellent articles that arouse the sentiments of the masses in keeping with the Party's intentions. He also brings up journalists to be the Party's reliable writers under his wings and takes meticulous care of every facet of their life and activity.

He has brought about constant improvement and upsurge in the press through his brilliant leadership.

No word, spoken or written, can express his mental energy and trouble devoted to this cause. And his love and benefit conferred upon the journalists are indeed endless.

The dear Comrade Kim Jong Il, who is adding new pages to the history of the Korean press upholding the high aim of the great leader Comrade Kim Il Sung, inspires us journalists to victory, glory, pleasure, happiness, hope and a bright future.

This book introduces some of the legendary stories about the dear leader, a great guide and teacher.

May 1983

CONTENTS

BRILLIANT GUIDANCE 1

Our Own Style 3

    Radio Signature Tune 3
    A New Article on Noble Personality 5
    To Give Wide Publicity to Typical Man of Our Time   8
    For Further Flowering of Political Essays 11
    The Art of Radio Speech of Our Own Style 14

Boldly and Ambitiously 19

    Ambitious Edition 19
    A Great Agitation Campaign on the Economic Front 21
    A Great Campaign to Give Publicity to Bumper Crops 24
    Three Picture Books 28

New Initiative 32

    In the Early Days of a Strong Popular Movement . . 32
    Inducing People to Follow the Example of Unassuming Heroes 35
    Giving Prominence to the Three-Revolution Team . . 37

Proposing the Idea of Emulating the Heroes of Classical
　　　Works 40

　　　Intensive Telecast of *Song of Comradeship* 43

Personally Standing in the Forefront 46

　　　During the Sixth Congress of the Workers' Party of
　　　Korea 46

　　　On the Eve of the Celebration Meeting 49

　　　This Is How the TV Broadcast Started 52

　　　Counting the Korean Pepper Bushes with a Journalist　55

　　　Taking the Place of a Reporter 58

　　　At the Opening Ceremony of the Children's Palace . 61

　　　On the Site of Video-tape Recording 65

　　　To Ensure Promptness of Information 67

Energetic and Meticulous Guidance 71

　　　The First Stereophoto of the Great Leader 71

　　　For an Editorial of Great Weight 73

　　　Three-Colour Ball-Pen Marks 76

　　　Till the Finishing Touch Is Given to a Travelogue . . 77

　　　"Press the Shutter When You Are Sure of Success" . 79

　　　Correcting a Mistake in the Notebook for News
　　　Coverage 82

　　　330 Famous Songs 84

Regarding a Small Thing as Important 87

　　　"The Train Broadcast Is Very Important" 87

    Supporting New Buds 90
    Seeing the Manuscripts for Announcers 93
    Announcers' Attire 95
    Letting Cars Take a Roundabout Way to Provide Quiet Working Conditions for Journalists 96

GREAT LOVE 99

Giving Prominence to Pressmen 101

    "Those Who Write in Accordance with the Party's Intention Are Heroes" 101
    Highly Praising Even a Small Success 103
    On New Year's Day 105
    Deep Concern for Establishment of the Broadcast Day 107

To Train Journalists Faithful to the Party 111

    A Copy of the Great Leader's Work Presented to an Official 111
    Journalists Must Read Books More Than Anyone Else 113
    Until They Have Grown Up into Editorial Writers .. 116
    "Make Yourself a Prominent Woman Journalist" .. 119
    Affection for an Announcer 122
    Concern for Training the Reserve of Journalists ... 126

For Better Working Conditions 129

    Offering a Choice 129

3

Concern over a Cameraman's Legwork	131
A New Building Sprang Up on the Potong River	133
He Sent a Special Plane	135
Warmth of Care Reaches a Far-off Continent	136

The Sun Shines in Every Nook and Corner of Life ... 139

Concern about the Meals of Journalists	139
To Give Them Even a Brief Rest	142
Holding an Umbrella	143
With the Feeling of a Father Desirous to Give One More	145
An Anecdote about the Dwellings of the Party Paper Journalists	147
Wedding Banquet of an Editor	149
An Entrance Certificate Permeated with His Affection	152

Guiding to Make Political Integrity Immortal ... 155

"But They Have Still Twenty to Thirty Years to Write"	155
To Keep Flowers in Bloom	157
The Dinner Arranged in Honour of a Newsman of the Party Paper on His 60th Birthday	160
Lasting Creative Enthusiasm	161
A Reporter Saved Miraculously from the Jaws of Death	163
Grief over the Death of Reporters	167
Awarding an Order to the Bereaved Child of a War Correspondent	169

BRILLIANT GUIDANCE

OUR OWN STYLE

Radio Signature Tune

Daybreak in the land of morning calm, the Juche Korea.

With the first glimpse of morning light the melody of *Song of General Kim Il Sung*, the immortal revolutionary hymn, rings out on the air.

Every morning our people rise and begin the day's routine with loyal hearts, hearing this great revolutionary hymn and feeling greatly proud of living and working in Korea, under the guidance of the great leader Comrade Kim Il Sung.

The melody of *Song of General Kim Il Sung* has now become our radio signature tune at the suggestion and as an expression of the high aim of the dear leader Comrade Kim Jong Il who is eager to give a distinctive characteristic to our broadcast as the voice of Juche Korea which is making the revolution under the guidance of the great leader Comrade Kim Il Sung.

A signature tune is something that identifies a radio. It is an important element which defines the character of a radio.

But the melody of *Spring Song* had served as our signature tune until only several years ago. This song is lyrical and awakens people to a deep thought.

The dear leader, always seeing everything with an innovator's eye and grasping the developing reality and the aspirations of our people, got the old signature tune replaced with the melody of *Song of General Kim Il Sung*.

On April 25, 1965, on his return from a long trip to a far-off country, the dear leader came to inspect the Radio and TV Broadcasting Committee, without even stopping to break the longstanding fatigue of the journey abroad.

Very much pleased to see again the broadcasting officials at work, in good health after an absence, he recollected his experience in the foreign country with deep emotions.

He said he had felt more keenly during the foreign trip that our socialist motherland was a good land to live in, a silk-embroidered land which is blessed with good mountains and clear water, gold, silver and other mineral wealth, and which fully provides a free and cultured life for the people who threw off the shackles of exploitation and oppression. He exhorted that our radio should be good at educating people in socialist patriotism and, in particular, broadcast many songs about the socialist motherland, and instil in the minds of the working people the sense of national pride of living in great happiness under the guidance of the great leader.

To this end, he said, it was necessary to change the signature tune before anything else. He went on to say:

"The character of our radio signature tune now in use is dull.

"Our broadcast is the voice of our Party which is guided by the leader, the voice of Juche Korea. So the signature tune which identifies the beginning of our radio programmes must naturally be a melody associated with the leader.

"It would be advisable to adopt as signature tune the melody of *Song of General Kim Il Sung*, the immortal revolutionary hymn which is sung with feelings of high respect for him not only by our people but all the people throughout the world."

His words reminded the officials that our country was indeed good, and they understood the true meaning of his earnest instruction to broadcast many songs of the socialist motherland.

They were amazed at the unusual intelligence of the dear leader who, thinking of the effect of the signature tune on mass education, took a bold step to change it to which no one had yet given attention while hearing it every morning for scores of years.

At his suggestion the tune of *Spring Song* was immediately replaced with the melody of *Song of General Kim Il Sung*, the immortal revolutionary hymn, which is now ringing out all over the world.

The dear leader also got the TV signature tune to be changed likewise.

This is how our radio has acquired more distinct characteristics and how it has become capable of contributing better to imbuing our people with the national pride of living and working in the socialist motherland established by him.

A New Article on Noble Personality

One day in April 1981, the dear leader Comrade Kim Jong Il gave an assignment to newspapermen of the *Rodong Sinmun* to write an article on great trust the respected leader Comrade Kim Il Sung had placed in Comrade Kang Yong Chang, an old intellectual, and on his warm love for the man.

Comrade Kang Yong Chang was a longstanding intellectual who had become a leading revolutionary official in the invariable confidence of the respected leader and had remained firm and loyal to the Party and the leader until the last moment of his life.

The journalists of the Party paper excitedly collected the

necessary materials on the great leader's consideration for him and drafted an article entitled, *Love Is Like the Sunshine*, (an account of confidence and love shown by the great leader to Comrade Kang Yong Chang and his family).

Having read the first galley proof, the dear leader clearly showed how to correct the article. He said that Comrade Kang Yong Chang was an old intellectual who had received a great deal of consideration from the leader, so that the article must give a good account of his personal relations with the leader.

This instruction offered the key to the composition of the article on the noble personality of the great leader and served as an essential guide to writing such articles.

Dealing with this subject had become a new journalistic trend in our country while education in loyalty to the Party and the leader developed in depth. Since the first days of this trend many a journalist handled such articles, often talking about the noble personality of the respected leader or the story line of reverence for him, but none of them had ever given thought to the matter of representing the human relations. This question was brought to light by the brilliant intelligence and clairvoyance of the dear leader who has inherited the noble communist personality of the great leader who, with unequalled, genuine love for the people and the sense of revolutionary ethics, approaches every one of his men as his revolutionary comrade.

An article which deals with the high virtue of the respected leader aims at describing his noble personality by giving an account of his trust and great care for the revolutionary fighters. This kind of writing should naturally give an account of the solid human relations between the leader and his revolutionary men.

Shown the absolutely correct way to write the article on the noble personality by the dear leader, the journalists confidently began to revise the draft.

The newspaper assigned more reporters to the task of covering the facts, as a step to reinforce the writers who were directly in charge of the article. The reporters tried to find out all the people who might know the facts of the great leader having guided and taken care of Comrade Kang Yong Chang.

Meanwhile, not taking his mind off the matter even after showing the way to revise the article, the dear leader gave an instruction to the relevant institution to offer the Party paper reporters information on the noble personality of the great leader in relation to Comrade Kang Yong Chang. With this valuable new information in hand, the writers got down to the task again and succeeded in revising the article, giving a profound and vivid picture on the line of human relationship.

The rewritten article bore a new title, *Noble Love That Made a Longstanding Intellectual's Life Brilliant*, and a subtitle, *An Account of the Great Leader Training Comrade Kang Yong Chang into Revolutionized Intellectual, a Leadership Official of the Country*.

The dear leader went over the article and then returned it to the newspaper on July 9 and got it carried on the same day.

On publication the article won a great response. The public were deeply impressed by the great trust and love of the respected leader shown to the intellectual throughout his life.

The journalists became convinced by this writing that articles dealing with the leader's noble personality should be handled on the main line of human relationship between the leader and his men.

On the morning when the article was carried in the *Rodong Sinmun*, the great leader Comrade Kim Il Sung recollected the life of Comrade Kang Yong Chang at a meeting of the Political Bureau of the Party Central Committee. Quoting from the information given in the paper, he explained the fact that he had trusted the man and how firm the man had been in upholding and defending the Party and the leader in the difficult years and how hard he had struggled to implement Party policies. The great leader instructed that every one of our people must follow the man's example.

This is how a living model was created of the articles dealing with the leader's noble personality, under the intelligent guidance and meticulous care of the dear leader Comrade Kim Jong Il who not only clarified the fundamental principle of writing such articles but took measures for the collection of necessary materials.

Since then, this type of writing has greatly improved its qualities by profoundly describing the human relationship between the leader and his men, and crystallized into a unique trend of our own style capable of truly contributing to the education of people in loyalty to the Party and the leader.

To Give Wide Publicity to Typical Man of Our Time

The July 27, 1976 issue of the *Rodong Sinmun* carried an article entitled, *He Will Loyally Follow a Single Road Forever*, illustrated with a picture of the great leader standing arm in arm with Comrade An Dal Su.

The article gave an account of how under the great leader's loving care Comrade An Dal Su had become a revolutionary who defended our Party's position on the agricultural front, and what was the conviction that had made him invariably loyal throughout the trying years.

One summer day in 1976 during his on-the-spot guidance

to South Hwanghae Province, the great leader Comrade Kim Il Sung met Labour Hero Comrade An Dal Su, chairman of the management board of the Sowon Cooperative Farm in Pyoksong County.

Sitting in his rushing car he acknowledged the saluting labour hero. The great leader stopped the car and had a long cordial talk with the hero on the wayside under the scorching sun.

Knowing that the man was very sorry to leave him at the moment, the great leader had a memorable picture taken with the man holding the man's arm in his. This bright picture which was taken in Sowon Plain that day gave a glimpse of this proud age when the great leader trusts the people and the people believe in him and follow him. It clearly showed the source of the unconquerable strength of our Party and the unshakable faith and will of our people.

The dear leader arranged the article about Comrade An Dal Su by sending reporters of the Party paper to the place.

The Party newspapermen, excited, quickly collected the necessary information and wrote an article of one page and a half in a short time.

The article met with a great response from the readers who were powerfully encouraged to implement the idea of the great leader with a firm determination to uphold it without yielding to any trials and difficulties just as Comrade An Dal Su had done. This patently proved that education by the example of a typical man of our time who is infinitely loyal to the great leader, had a great influence and attractive power, just as the leader had intended.

The dear leader showed the method of further enhancing the cognitive and educative role of the articles to influence people by positive examples, in conformity with the new historical period when the cause of modelling the whole society on the Juche idea is gaining momentum and when a radical change is taking place in the ideological and spiritual features of our people.

The dear Comrade Kim Jong Il said:

"**The *Rodong Sinmun* must give ample space to the articles for education by means of positive examples.**

"**The newspaper must deal with many people who met the leader like the chairman of the management board of the Changjin Fishermen's Cooperative in Tongchon County, Kangwon Province as well as many heroes.**"

The typical men of our time are represented by true revolutionaries who silently work to implement the great leader's instructions for ten years, twenty years and through all their lives with feelings of ardent respect for him. Therefore, giving prominence to these typical men is an effective method of imbuing people with loyalty to the Party and the leader.

The dear leader had a noble aim of educating a large number of people through the very influence of such a typical man when he personally arranged the article about Comrade An Dal Su.

Since then the Party paper and other press media began to deal consistently and systematically with typical men of our time who are boundlessly loyal to the great leader, and a new turn has taken place in dealing with positive examples.

The articles which handle these typical people and impress the readers immensely, have enhanced their cognitive and educative role without precedent in training the Party membership and working people to be boundlessly loyal to the Party and their leader.

This is how the article on positive examples to educate people in our own style, an article which appeared for the first time in our press at the suggestion of the great leader when the Chollima Movement was initiated following the completion of socialist reorganization of the production relations in town and country, is now in its heyday under the wise leadership of the dear leader Comrade Kim Jong Il.

For Further Flowering of Political Essays

At the beginning of the 1980s the Party paper's political essays became a special highlight of our press media.

Political essays in our country developed as an independent trend under the intelligent guidance of the great leader Comrade Kim Il Sung in the early 1960s when an upswing was taking place in the Chollima Movement. They met with a great response from the broad masses of the readers.

This style of writing has further flourished owing to the outstanding policy of the dear leader Comrade Kim Jong Il and under his energetic guidance with the advent of 1980s when a new revolutionary upswing was being initiated by the historic Sixth Congress of the Workers' Party of Korea.

Political essays including *New Song of Automation, Korean Pride, People Sing of the Leader, Great Traditions, Comradeship, Korea's Mettle, Revolutionary Conviction, Legendary Hero,* and *Strength of the Workers' Party* gripped the hearts of the masses, moved them deeply and won great sympathies from among them because of the fresh and original titles, the importance of their seeds and subjects, the philosophical profundity of the thoughts and vivid facts they dealt with, and their powerful expressions.

In this way the political essays carried in the Party paper have become a most effective ideological weapon which represents our Party's authoritative voice on the acutest socio-political questions of our time and expresses the aspirations of our people. These essays have evolved a distinct style of their own as a journalistic trend which educates the masses to breathe with the times and encourages them to work zealously for the revolution and construction in the spirit of the times.

The new flowering of political essays which marks a turning point in the annals of our Party press would have been inconceivable, from the very start through all stages of its development, without the meticulous and energetic guidance of the dear Comrade Kim Jong Il.

With a clear insight into the reality which was vibrant with the spirit of the new times around the historic Sixth Congress of the Workers' Party of Korea held in October 1980 and into our people's aspirations, the dear leader proposed a new political essay campaign for the Party paper and took measures to ensure success in the campaign.

The two years and more since the start of the political essay campaign were a period of worthwhile struggle to develop this style of writing into full flowering. These were glorious annals adorned brilliantly with the dear leader's meticulous and energetic guidance and great efforts.

The dear leader has not only given instructions on each of the titles, seeds, subjects and thoughts of the essays but has gone over the manuscripts in person, making necessary corrections even to individual expressions to make them perfect.

How meticulous guidance he has given to each of the essays and how hard he has elaborated on them can be illustrated by how an essay *Revolutionary Conviction* was written.

The *Revolutionary Conviction* was indeed an essay which owed its perfection to his elaborate teaching on its seed, theme, thought, materials and expressions and to his personal corrections on these matters.

Giving the assignment to write this essay on March 21, 1981, the dear leader Comrade Kim Jong Il instructed:

"There is the need to write a good political essay which deals with the viewpoint of a revolutionary on human life."

The revolutionary point of view on human life has been an urgent question historically, and particularly for the revolutionaries of our time. The arduous and complicated Korean revolution with the task of reunifying the country in unceasing confrontation with the US imperialists on the Military Demarcation Line urgently required our people to equip themselves with a revolutionary outlook on human life. Historical experience shows that people without a correct revolutionary viewpoint on human life cannot withstand the grim and arduous trials of revolution and may betray the Party and the revolution at the crucial moment.

On many occasions in connection with the task of writing this essay, the dear leader talked to the officials on a number of instructive and meaningful subjects—the question of revolutionary conviction and features of a true revolutionary, the question of a revolutionary and death, that is, questions which concern the revolutionary viewpoint on human life. His words clearly showed the subject matter and the core of the essay and the way to elaborate coherently on its serious subject.

The revolutionary viewpoint on human life was a philosophical question which involved huge and profound content, and it was not until then that the Party paper put this question to the fore. But the writers were able from the outset to grasp the revolutionary conviction, the essence of the viewpoint on human life, raise the points of arguments boldly and thrash them out because they had been informed of the explicit intention of the dear leader, his original and perfect theory of the viewpoint on human life, the core of the question and the method of amplification. After ceaseless thinking, discussion and repeated improvement, the writers finished the essay on April 9, 1981, some time after they received the assignment from the dear leader.

Despite the heavy pressure of work, the dear leader went over the first galley proof of the essay again and again, underlining well-composed passages and making corrections on a number of points until it became complete, and then he highly appraised the essay.

The political essay *Revolutionary Conviction* won a great response on its publication. It contributed greatly to instilling in the minds of the Party membership and working people a firmer revolutionary conviction and determination to uphold the banner of revolution consistently in all circumstances.

All the political essays which were carried in the Party paper and met with great response, owed their seeds and perfection to the tireless efforts of the dear leader just as the essay *Revolutionary Conviction* did.

Today, when political essays have entered a heyday under the energetic guidance and meticulous care of the dear leader, we, journalists, recollect the road our political essays have traversed with a high sense of pride and pay high respect to him who has brought about this great change.

The Art of Radio Speech of Our Own Style

One day in September 1968, the tenth anniversary of the founding of the Nampo and Haeju Revolutionary Schools was to be celebrated augustly in the presence of the great leader at the playground of the Nampo Revolutionary School.

In the spacious, clean ground the schoolchildren in neat uniforms and with flower bundles in hand were waiting impatiently for the arrival of the great leader. There was also a radio announcer on a mission to report on the spot the news of the day's function.

The announcer was checking his readiness to ensure success in the important political function which was to be attended by the great leader.

He happened to see the dear leader Comrade Kim Jong Il approaching the spot where his tape recorders were set.

In irresistible excitement and delight at the sight of the dear leader whom he had been so eager to see, the announcer stood up and courteously greeted him.

The dear leader with a broad smile on his face warmly shook hands with the announcer, confirmed if he was to relay the report of the function, emphasized the importance of his mission and his great responsibility, and then asked the name of the announcer. Hearing his answer, the dear leader said that he was very glad to have met him in person, though he had known of him on the air.

Looking affectionately at the announcer, the dear leader said:

"If the radio is to fulfil its mission as an ideological weapon of our Party, announcers must enhance their role.

"Announcers must not think that all that they have to do to perform their duty is to read just the writings of journalists. They must become propagandists who spread far and wide the voice of our Party by means of a revolutionary art of speech. They must become fighters who staunchly defend Party policies and powerfully mobilize the masses in their implementation.

"Every word they speak before their microphones must grasp the hearts of the masses of people, inspire them strongly, scare the enemy like a bomb, and express the mettle, noble thoughts and emotions and aspirations of our people who are working for the revolution and struggling."

These words of the dear leader clarified the place and mission of announcers and provided the key to the Juche-oriented diction suited for our cultured language. The instruction has brought about a new change in the standpoint, posture, ideological viewpoint and the way of thinking of the announcers who speak to the public through microphones. It gave the announcers a new understanding that the work of creating a diction based on our cultured language was something more than a technical and practical matter of raising just the level of skill in eloquence, that every word they speak must convey the spirit of our era of revolution and struggle and the noble thoughts, emotions and aspirations of our people.

On the matter of intensifying the training to create the diction based on our cultured language, the dear Comrade Kim Jong Il instructed:

"**Inanimate, inert and dull speech would be unable to rouse people vigorously to the revolutionary struggle and the work of construction.**

"**All announcers must train themselves energetically in the diction suited for cultured language in accordance with the leader's instructions and master the revolutionary and popular art of speech.**"

Art of speech based on the cultured language means one which is based on the language which has developed in Pyongyang, the revolutionary capital, and its vicinity and which is spoken by the working masses.

That day, the dear leader explained in detail the important questions arising in the creation of such a diction, the principles which all announcers must follow, and later on he gave meticulous guidance to the implementation of these principles.

One day in February 1974, he was listening to the radio, while directing the struggle for grand socialist construction. He noticed the shortcoming of some announcers speaking inanimately, wholly intent on the technical aspect of their speech. He reminded the officials concerned of the shortcoming and said as follows:

"**Appeal and militant character of broadcast must not**

be weakened allegedly to give tender differentiation to the speech....

"The present situation which is vibrant with the struggle for grand socialist construction requires a forceful language in radio propaganda, too, which can give the implication of the spirit to push forward, just as the magnificent circumstances in the postwar reconstruction period demanded something more than a beautiful speech. Announcers' voice itself must give an impulse to rush forward."

With a clear insight into the most serious weakness in the manner of radio speech, the dear leader showed how to eliminate the weakness and then took measures to ensure that the announcers spoke militantly and appealingly, in meeting the need of the times when grand socialist construction was under way.

Knowing that announcers' manner of speech was lagging behind the times because they were cooped up in the radio studio isolated from the vibrant reality, the dear leader saw to it that the announcers went through the thrill of socialist construction. They went out to the Hwanghae Iron Works, the Komdok and Ryongyang Mines, the Yanghwa and Sinpo Fishery Stations where the flags of big catches were flying, the Chongsan and Hamju Plains where the song of rich harvest resounded, to feel in their hearts the high spirits and fighting mettle of the working class and farmers of our time who were making miraculous new successes and innovations, displaying loyalty to the great leader and the Party.

Moreover, quite a few announcers were included in the broadcasting detachments which were sent to the Huichon Machine-Tool Factory and the Kumsong Tractor Plant. They powerfully encouraged the workers there to a new struggle to increase production, by means of their militant and stirring broadcast.

In this course the announcers were able to develop a strongly militant and appealing manner of speech capable of expressing the pulse of the times and the revolutionary spirit of the people.

Today our announcers are vigorously spreading all around the voice of our Party by means of the diction of our own style. They owe this precisely to the dear leader who has given them energetic and meticulous guidance to implement brilliantly the great leader's idea of Juche-oriented diction based on cultured language.

BOLDLY AND AMBITIOUSLY

Ambitious Edition

On March 2, 1976, the Party paper was to report the on-the-spot guidance to Anju by the great leader Comrade Kim Il Sung.

The officials of the newspaper sent the reporters to the scene and got down to the arrangement of the editorial plan. Then they were waiting for the reporters to return, assuming that the remaining task was to edit information expected from the reporters.

At this very moment the dear leader Comrade Kim Jong Il acquainted himself with the preparations for the day's issue of the newspaper. Knowing that they were going to edit only the article on the great leader's on-the-spot guidance, he advised them to extend the mental horizon.

Referring to the matter of how to handle the report of the on-the-spot guidance given by the great leader to Anju, the dear leader said:

"The issue which is being prepared today must include the report of the leader's on-the-spot guidance to Anju and carry as a special item the news of the construction of Anju on its second and third pages.

"I wonder whether you have pictures of the whole view of Anju under construction....

"You must organize the work quickly and arrange the

special edition and report of the leader's on-the-spot guidance to Anju."

Anju is a beautiful modern town which has newly sprung up on the Chongchon River, whose construction was proposed by the great leader and carried out under his constant guidance and care.

The great leader inspected Anju city which had been built in a short time and provided basically with all modern amenities. He expressed great satisfaction at the excellently built streets.

The town was the pride of our time which had been built under the wise guidance of the respected leader out of his warm love for the working class. It was an impressively beautiful town which showed the greatness of the leader.

His on-the-spot guidance at the time was unusual in that it was something of a review of his own effort dedicated to the gigantic creation.

In this context the day's edition should have included these vivid facts, concentrating on the great leader's far-sighted plan of building local towns, his intelligent leadership to translate it into reality, his boundlessly warm love and great solicitude for our working class. But the editorial staff could not work out a plan of such magnitude in depth.

A number of reports on the great leader's on-the-spot guidance had been edited by that time, but there had never been such a special edition in which the first three pages of an issue were devoted to the information of an on-the-spot guidance.

The dear leader guided the editorial staff to widen their narrow view and give the greatest prominence to the report of the great leader's activity in keeping with the great significance of the construction of Anju so that the greatness of the respected leader would be vivid. He made sure that the editors laid out the edition ambitiously and boldly so that the great leader's wise guidance, noble personality, and high popular features would grip the heart of everyone.

Hearing the bold and innovative plan of the dear leader for a special edition covering up to the third page including the report of the great leader's on-the-spot guidance to Anju, the editors were overjoyed.

Full of confidence and enthusiasm, the Party paper officials immediately organized articles for the special edition.

The result was that the first page of the issue carried the report of the great leader's on-the-spot guidance and the picture of his inspection of Anju city, and the second and third pages included an article on the great love shown by the leader for the construction of Anju, articles which introduced the new town and the struggle of the town builders, and many photographs which offered a whole view of the town, filling up the space on a largest scale.

Thus the great leader's on-the-spot guidance to Anju was reported in bold relief, and another new example was created in the report of the respected leader's on-the-spot guidance.

A Great Agitation Campaign on the Economic Front

In autumn 1973. There was a very rich crop in our country under the brilliant rays of the great leader's theses on the socialist rural question.

Giving the task of reaping and threshing the rich crop in time, the great leader instructed that more lorries and tractors necessary for the task be produced for the countryside.

Upon the great leader's instructions, officials of the press discussed how to conduct press activity to contribute to finishing threshing as soon as possible in all parts of the country.

They were earnest and racking their brains for a bright idea unsuccessfully.

The dear leader Comrade Kim Jong Il again showed them the way clear enough to implement the respected leader's instructions successfully as he has always done to help and guide in detail the press media to accept the instructions correctly and carry them out.

On November 3, 1973, the dear leader organized a great agitation campaign on the economic front to finish threshing and produce the required number of lorries and tractors.

Referring to the need for all the press media to concentrate on the task of threshing and putting the production of lorries and tractors on a normal basis during the campaign, the dear leader said:

"The newspaper must subordinate the first four pages to this task. We must conduct mass agitation and education with concentrated efforts like this."

His words were a magnificent declaration which initiated a great agitation campaign on the economic front which was unprecedented in the annals of our Party press.

Since then the Party press has unfolded a new history of a great agitation campaign on the economic front, which was qualitatively distinct from the one in the preceding period in its scale and content, form and method.

The dear leader gave the direction of this campaign, and for its execution he organized strong forces into on-the-spot report and propaganda teams, broadcasting detachments and mobile art troupes of the provincial broadcast and sent them to threshing grounds and automobile and tractor factories.

The reporters and editorial workers who went off their office rooms to the workers and farmers, powerfully inspired the masses by means of diverse forms of agitation, eating and sleeping among them and helping them in their work just as the anti-Japanese guerrillas did. They wrote forceful and vigorous articles capable of imbuing people's hearts with ardent feelings of loyalty and launched an uninterrupted report and propaganda campaign.

In particular, the broadcasting detachments and the mobile art troupes of the provincial broadcast made every "battle" site vibrant with ardent loyalty and encouraged the people to dynamic struggle on the labour front by using various forms and means such as radio political essays, radio soiree, and mobile oral agitation.

All propaganda and agitation media were mobilized in agitation to increase production, and all newspapers and radios devoted most of their space and time to the support of the struggle for threshing and for the production of lorries and tractors.

In this period the *Rodong Sinmun*, the Party paper, devoted the first four of its six pages to this agitation, and other newspapers, too, dedicated the first three of their four pages respectively. In particular, the dailies of North and South Pyongan Provinces and North and South Hwanghae Provinces devoted all their efforts to agitation for increased production.

The Central Radio continued with intensive broadcast without being bound to the fixed timetable, under the title, *Let us become honourable victors in harvesting by working assiduously and aggressively with the attitude of masters of the revolution, Produce tractors and lorries more and faster for the cooperative farms which have grown rich crops*, etc.

The agitation campaign to increase production which was directly organized and guided by the dear leader, involved all the reporters and editorial staffs, and all the press media served this campaign with all their efforts.

This campaign was indeed a large-scale lightning operation which employed the finish-one-by-one tactics in agitation for increased production.

While pushing forward the agitation campaign like lightning by mobilizing all means of propaganda and agitation and using all forms and methods, the dear leader saw to it that the agitation efforts were concentrated on the vital links to finish them one by one and prove the immediate effectiveness of agitation.

The great agitation campaign on the economic front put the whole country in the heat of struggle at once and brought about a great upswing in production and construction.

The automobile and tractor output in November that year showed a remarkable increase, and from mid-November the threshing work was completed in one province after another.

The reality clearly showed that the agitation for increased production organized personally by the dear leader in 1973 was a powerful means capable of effecting unprecedented upswing in production and construction by gripping the hearts of the masses and increasing their revolutionary enthusiasm to an unusual height and by rousing them vigorously to the implementation of the great leader's instructions and Party policies.

A Great Campaign to Give Publicity to Bumper Crops

In 1974 there was an unusually rich crop in every part of our countryside. The well-cultivated fields of our cooperatives were swaying with thriving crops, and the hearts of the people were throbbing with boundless joy of having grown bumper crops.

The dear leader Comrade Kim Jong Il worked out a bold plan for the newspapers to give wide publicity to the unprecedented bumper crops in order to prove patently the sagacity of the respected leader's guidance and the validity of our Party's agrarian policy and demonstrate the brilliant victory of the great theses on the socialist rural question.

In early September that year the dear leader gave instructions to the Party paper to carry articles and pictures of the rich crop and explained in concrete terms that they should continue with the project efficiently in the period ahead.

But the editorial staff who were following the established practice and sticking to their outdated experience thought that it would be enough if they organized a few special editions on the rich crops. So they were too conservative and sluggish in arranging the work.

In these very circumstances, in mid-October the same year, the dear leader personally arranged a campaign for the newspaper to give wide publicity to the rich crop.

He said that we had grown unusually rich crops that year when the rest of the world was worried about crop failure. Pointing out the need for the newspaper to launch a big propaganda campaign on the question of agriculture, the dear leader said:

"We must concentrate our efforts on the propaganda for the great success in our agriculture for a fortnight from now on....

"Newspapers must give large-letter titles to this matter and highlight it.

"From tomorrow on you had better give special prominence to the agrarian question....

"For the present you have to give less space to political articles and concentrate on this question and launch a food propaganda campaign, that is, an agriculture propaganda campaign."

That day the dear leader explained in detail the purpose and necessity of this propaganda campaign, the direction and principles of the report campaign, the content of articles, the methods of covering the news, the forms of edition and so on.

His policy of agriculture propaganda campaign which was to concentrate on the report of rich crops as a special topic, was a bold and ambitious editorial campaign the like of which they had never heard of or experienced. It was an innovative proposition to do away boldly with the outdated notion of the editorial workers and their outdated work method.

On that very day the Party paper editors arranged a special edition covering the second and third pages on the rich rice and maize crops, as a step to implement the dear leader's instructions.

The next day the dear leader re-emphasized the need for the newspaper to go on giving prominence to agriculture. He specified the vegetable crop situation at the third sub-workteam, the third vegetable workteam of the Oryu Cooperative Farm, Sadong District, Pyongyang City, which he had been informed of, as the highlight to be reported by the *Rodong Sinmun*, and selected the seed for the article and also pointed out other objects of news coverage. Picking up the layout of the day's issue and two of the rich-crop pictures, he even fixed the sizes of the pictures to be edited, one in full-length of the page and the other in quadruple columns.

Receiving the pictures selected by the dear leader, the editorial staff became amazed at his choice.

The full-length-column picture of a vegetable field which stretched as far as the horizon, and the other one showing the farmers weighing and rejoicing over their cabbages as large as bunches of hemp, were a demonstration of success in vegetable cultivation in our country.

This bold idea of the dear leader was put into effect in the October 18 issue of the *Rodong Sinmun:* the second page carried an article on the all-time high per-*chongbo* rice yield together with the picture of the rich crop cultivated with machines by the Chongsan Cooperative Farm, under a heavy-letter title, *Brilliant Realization of the Leader's Far-Sighted Plan*; and the third page was totally devoted to the articles on the bumper vegetable crop grown by the Oryu, Rihyon, and Changchon Cooperative Farms, Pyongyang

City under the heading, *Unprecedentedly Rich Vegetable Crop Grown under the Rays of the Theses on the Socialist Rural Question*.

Commenting on that issue of the newspaper, the dear Comrade Kim Jong Il remarked in delight:

"The leader was satisfied with the edition of the report of the vegetable crop given in today's Party paper, saying that it was excellent."

Conveying the great leader's words of high praise and encouraging the editorial staff of the Party paper, the dear leader reiterated that during the 18-day food propaganda campaign, the agriculture propaganda campaign, the paper should devote every day at least one page, or two if necessary, to the agrarian question even if there were political functions.

According to his instructions, the Party paper organized one or two pages of special or intensive editions every day for half a month, dealing with proud news of abundant crops of rice, maize, vegetables and all other farm products in the plains, intermediate zones and highlands, in diverse forms of articles such as report, introduction of experiences, visitors' accounts, on-the-spot news and well-sized photographs. For comparative effect, the paper also edited information on the agricultural crisis, the food crisis, in south Korea and capitalist countries, articles exposing their reactionary agrarian policies and their aftereffects.

The *Rodong Sinmun*'s great agriculture propaganda campaign which was organized and guided personally by the dear leader was, indeed, a song of high praise for the greatness of the respected leader who brought the bumper crop to this land. It was also an august declaration of the brilliant victory of our Party's agrarian policy. It was also a barrage that hit hard the imperialists and the propaganda media on the payroll of the bourgeoisie, who maliciously slandered the socialist system of agriculture.

Three Picture Books

One summer day in 1974 the dear leader Comrade Kim Jong Il was informed of the fact that the great leader Comrade Kim Il Sung had asked if there was a big picture book introducing our country. Making up his mind to make such a book for the great leader, he immediately organized an operation to edit it.

The dear leader called in the officials in charge of this matter. Speaking of the need to publish three picture books on political, economic and cultural affairs, people's lives and natural scenery of our country, he said:

"Book One of the pictorial series should handle the revolutionary traditions, Book Two socialist construction, and Book Three the culture and art and natural scenery of our country."

This was a plan of publishing unprecedentedly large picture books.

With a smile the dear leader asked the overjoyed officials how long it would take them to produce these picture books.

The officials made a bold estimate and answered that they would try to do it within three to four years.

At this the dear leader burst into a roar of laughter and said that in three to four years' time Chollima Korea would take on a new look and that he was afraid the picture books would become outdated even before they could see the light.

The officials could say nothing.

After a short while of thinking the dear leader said confidently that he would like to get it done in one year, in twelve months, to be precise.

Such a bold decision to publish so big picture books in a

year would have been inconceivable for any other people than the dear leader who is peerlessly audacious and endowed with an unequalled ability to push forward the revolution.

The Foreign Languages Publishing House got down to the task, determined to finish it within the time set by the dear leader.

Many were the difficulties that stood in their way.

Taking all these and other factors into account, the dear leader worked out a careful plan of operations which closely integrated the whole process of photographing, writing, editing and printing, and then gave efficient leadership to push the work rapidly.

Once the work of photographing, the first and foremost process, got stuck.

Making up his mind to resolve the colossal problem of photographing by mobilizing Party organizations, the dear leader gave urgent instructions to the local Party organizations, telling them to help cameramen with all their efforts.

The large-scale operation to photograph more than 500 objects in some 80 cities and counties throughout the country began in this way.

It was when one cameramen's team arrived at Chongjin to take pictures of the revolutionary battle sites and places associated with revolutionary activities. They were met by a local Party official who had come with a few buses and was waiting for them.

They did not know what all that meant, and then they were wrapped up in excitement at the words of the official who had explained that they had been instructed by the dear leader to wait, ready to ensure that the cameramen's team were beginning their work on their arrival.

For ten days from that time on, the cameramen were able to take good pictures under the best working conditions, travelling hundreds of miles with loyal hearts through Rajin,

Sonbong, Onsong, Hoeryong and other places.

Such was not the case only in North Hamgyong Province. The Hwanghae Iron Works saw to it that magnificent pictures were taken of every furnace pouring forth molten iron, and the management officials of Lake Manpung, the vast man-made lake, arranged for the cameramen heart-swelling scenes of the outflux of the lifegiving water which would irrigate hundreds and thousands of *chongbo* of rice paddies.

Meantime, in the air above Pyongyang airplanes were flying with the cameramen aboard, and near the shore of the Sea Kumgang, one of the beauty spots on the east coast, ships were ploughing the blue waves to ensure the cameramen's work.

Thus all the necessary pictures were taken only in a matter of two months.

The dear leader examined thousands of sheets of pictures one by one and selected several hundreds from among them for the editorial staff. When the editing process was over, he went carefully through the editor's copy of 1,000 pages six times over and over again, giving kind advice to the points overlooked even by the editors and experts in photography.

Under the energetic guidance of the dear leader the three picture books (*The Immortal Revolutionary Traditions, Socialist Construction in Chollima Korea* and *Juche Culture Flowering in the Beautiful Land*) which had been estimated to take them three to four years to finish, were published in less than a year.

Looking through the three picture books one by one, the great leader Comrade Kim Il Sung was greatly satisfied and highly appraised them; in particular he said that the *Juche Culture Flowering in the Beautiful Land* was the best.

The officials were stirred up to irresistible emotions and excitement at the great leader's high appreciation.

The three picture books which show the mighty look of

Chollima Korea owed their publication precisely to the peerless audacity, brilliant intelligence and tireless guidance of the dear leader rather than individual cameramen or editorial staff members.

NEW INITIATIVE

In the Early Days of a Strong Popular Movement

In Korea each revolutionary stage witnessed a strong popular movement which brought about great changes.

The period when grand monumental structures were built in every part of the country and the revolution was accelerated through the popular movement, is replete with unforgettable stories about the extraordinary wisdom and guidance of the Party and the leader.

Particularly the mass campaigns initiated in the 1970s are associated with beautiful and noble stories about the exceptional intelligence and outstanding guidance ability of the dear leader.

At the beginning of the 1970s, our country was vibrating with a vigorous forward movement to effect new changes. The revolutionary zeal of the masses and the demand of the times for further progress grew stronger as the days went by.

This reality urgently required further development of the ideological, technical and cultural revolutions.

One day in November 1975, the dear leader who clearly saw the mature demand of the revolution with extraordinary intelligence put forward a policy of briskly unfolding the Three-Revolution Red Flag Movement the great leader had already planned.

This movement proposed by the dear leader is a new type of popular campaign commensurate with a high stage of our revolution; it aims to step up the three revolutions, setting as a fighting slogan the ultimate goal of our Party to model the whole society on the Juche idea.

He saw to it that this movement was carried on powerfully under the militant slogan of "Let's meet the requirements of Juche in ideology, technology and culture!" He attached great significance to the role played by the Party paper *Rodong Sinmun* in conducting this movement as a campaign by all the people, and kindly led it to carry on brisk editing operations.

At that time he encouraged the workers of the Komdok Mine in the industrial branch and the farmers of Chongsan-ri in the agricultural branch to raise the first torchlight of the Three-Revolution Red Flag Movement, and then looked after the *Rodong Sinmun* so that it would become the standard-bearer of the struggle, the bugler for the advance, to rouse the whole nation and all the people to this movement.

Journalists of the Party paper went out to the Komdok Mine and Chongsan-ri according to the measure taken by the dear leader. There they met functionaries, workers and farmers to discuss the targets and ways for the movement and helped them work out detailed plans for lighting its first signal-fire and make preparations for it.

As a result, on December 1, 15 days after his initiation of this movement, the Komdok miners entered in it under the revolutionary slogan "Let's meet the requirements of Juche in ideology, technology and culture!"

At the meeting of employees they set high aims to be attained in the ideological, technical and cultural spheres, and made a firm resolve to carry them out. Then they called earnestly upon the workers, technicians and office men and women of industrial enterprises across the country to take part in this movement.

That night the dear leader examined the layout of the *Rodong Sinmun* which would report the Komdok miners' initiative in bold letters, and instructed to edit this historic event on an unprecedentedly big scale.

As a consequence, the *Rodong Sinmun* in its issue of December 2, 1975 covered four full pages—from the front to the fourth—with the news of Komdok miners.

The following day the paper also reported in its four full pages the news that the agricultural workers of Chongsan-ri had entered in this movement.

The paper edited in bold type the news of the workers in Pyongyang, Hamhung, Chongjin and other provincial seats, in the Hwanghae Iron Works, Ryongsong Machine Factory, Taean Electrical Machinery Plant and other enterprises, as well as the members of Rihyon, Ryongchon, Oguk and other cooperative farms throughout the country, who had joined in the movement.

Every day the Party paper gave wide publicity to the news of innovations in factories and farms all over the country, Komdok and Chongsan-ri included; they were printed in special and intensive editions or at the top on the front page.

Strong editorials and inspiring political essays appeared one after another, calling on the whole nation to enhance this movement.

Thanks to intensive propaganda carried on for nearly a month under the guidance of the dear leader, the whole country was vibrant with the movement and great progress was made in all domains of ideology, technology and culture.

This was the start of the grandiose onward movement by the entire people to reach the high peak of socialism and communism.

Indeed, the stirring days when the Three-Revolution Red Flag Movement began showed us the dear leader's traditional method of guidance whereby an example was set at a unit and generalized throughout the country; they were the impressive days when he skilfully and wisely led millions of the masses to struggle and innovation, by means of the *Rodong Sinmun*, a powerful ideological weapon of the Party.

Inducing People to Follow the Example of Unassuming Heroes

It was October 1979 when golden ears of rice were ceaselessly rolling in vast plains and even in ravines. Everyone was pleased with bumper crops, when the great leader found out unassuming heroes who had been working devotedly, meeting the Party's intentions in silence, as if he discovered jewels in the mud.

A few days later, the great leader convened an important meeting attended by the officials in the capital and from the provinces and invited these heroes to the meeting, where he made a really significant statement that our Republic was mighty and so was our Party because there were such numerous unassuming heroes and that everyone should follow their example of serving the Party and the revolution, the country and the people.

True to the great leader's high purpose, the dear leader proposed to launch a whole Party, nationwide movement to follow their example and induced the Party paper *Rodong Sinmun* to get this movement started.

As the first step, the dear leader got the Party paper to introduce widely the stories of unassuming heroes, and gave energetic guidance to the writing of articles about them.

So the journalists of this newspaper wrote in a few days an article about an unassuming hero under the title, *A Single Heart for the Party and the People*.

The dear leader, in spite of numerous claims on him, went over the two-page article, giving it finishing touches.

On publication the article won a widespread response among the readers.

The dear leader instructed that their reactions were reported in succession by the Party paper, and energetically guided it to write articles about other heroes and edit them conspicuously.

One day in late October of the same year, the dear leader who had looked through a Party paper article about another unassuming hero cast a new light on the seed of it and pointed out how to elaborate on it, assigning a task for it to be rewritten. Turning over the manuscript he had looked through, the writers felt a lump in their throats. It was because he marked off some passages which needed rewriting, and pointed out what should be emphasized, even revising some expressions.

The dear leader said:

"The account of Comrade Pak Yong Chol was not bold enough to show his struggle against the conservatists.

"The course of his invention of new techniques was by no means smooth; it was a process of a fierce struggle against die-hards. But the article is not giving a full account of the fact."

Bearing in mind this precious remark, the writers rewrote the article in a few hours as he had taught them. He went over the account on that very day when the Party paper journalists submitted it, and added finishing touches.

Besides, he fixed the specific dates for editing articles.

From October 27, therefore, articles on unassuming heroes were carried in the Party paper one after another. As he intended, these articles excited the whole country.

Much pleased with the fact that the articles were producing a great repercussion among all Party members and working people, he spoke highly of the journalists' efforts.

Soon after he made the example of unassuming heroes well known to the whole Party and nation, the dear leader planned to turn this movement into a mass campaign for ideological transformation and saw to it that the newspaper opened a forum for the readers to follow the example.

As a result, from November 11, 1979, the Party paper offered a whole page to the letters of determination from the broad masses every day under the fixed headlines, *Let's Follow the Example of Unassuming Heroes!* and *For the Party and the Leader, for the Country and the People.*

The readers' forum lasted some 140 days until March 31, 1980, and the letters sent to the forum in this period numbered more than 2,420,000, of which 2,367 were published.

Never before had there been such a large-scale forum in the history of the Party paper and our newspapers in general.

The movement to follow the example of the unassuming heroes has thus involved the whole Party and the whole society, attracted the masses with great force and touched their hearts.

Indeed, this movement started by the Party paper on the initiative of the dear leader has given a great impetus to our people's further advance and innovations in all spheres of their ideological and mental lives, economic and cultural construction and Party work, and is displaying its great value with each passing day.

Giving Prominence to the Three-Revolution Team

On December 20, 1976, the dear leader called a functionary into his office room and said:

"Since the *Rodong Sinmun* reflects the Party, it ought to become the forerunner in disseminating Party policy.

"From now on it should carry lots of materials on the three-revolution-team movement."

The three-revolution-team movement is a campaign initiated by the great leader in 1973 for the successful implementation of the line of the three revolutions, our Party's general line.

This is a new method of guiding the revolution combining political and ideological guidance with scientific and technical guidance to the three revolutions, enabling the higher echelons to help the lower echelons and rousing the masses of working people to accelerate these revolutions.

In order to step up this movement, the dear leader organized three-revolution teams with competent workers fully prepared politically and practically, as well as young intellectuals imbued with the Juche idea and armed with modern scientific and technical know-how, and sent them to all domains of the national economy.

Thanks to the zealous activity of the members of these teams sent by our Party, a really great advance was being made in the ideological, technical and cultural revolutions.

In order to highly appreciate the service they had rendered, the dear leader instructed that they should be introduced in the Party paper.

He repeatedly asked the Party paper officials to report on them widely on the previous day, December 19, and pointed out:

"The work of three-revolution teams can be reported mainly on the second page of the newspaper. Great importance must be attached to the news....

"The words 'working class' must necessarily be followed by the term 'three-revolution teams'. Whenever you deal with different subjects, you should put in a word about these teams."

All editing staffs learning what he had said looked at one another in admiration.

Until then it was a usual practice to edit on the second page the reports on the great leader's revolutionary activities.

articles of his virtues, political essays, editorials and other major articles.

His instructions to devote the second page to the news of three-revolution teams implied his high intention to introduce their achievements in a most conspicuous place of the newspaper.

Having received his instructions, the reporters and editorial staff scrupulously organized the work to disseminate the achievements and experiences of these teams.

The Party paper set a fixed headline for this purpose and edited their news on the second page so conspicuously as to catch the eyes of readers.

In addition, it put a subheading, *Workers (or Farmers) and Three-Revolution-Team Members of the Factories (or Farms)* just under the headlines of all articles introducing industrial enterprises and cooperative farms so that the readers could see them at a glance when they turned over the front page.

In this way an epochal change began to take place under his meticulous guidance in giving publicity to the three-revolution-team members.

The Party paper and other mass media are widely introducing and propagating the achievements of the teams as well as the rich experience gained in the three revolutions. By so doing they are inspiring all the team members throughout the country to fulfil their mission and duty with a high pride as the vanguards of the three revolutions, making great contribution to the strengthening and development of this movement.

Proposing the Idea of Emulating the Heroes of Classical Works

It was December 20, 1972. On that evening the dear leader summoned a leading official of the *Minju Choson*. He explained in detail how to improve the edition of this newspaper and why it should organize well the work of emulating the heroes of revolutionary literary works.

He pointed out:

"While seeing *Sea of Blood* and *The Flower Girl*, every spectator feels a strong sympathy with their heroes and heroines, an urge to make the revolution daringly like them. Precisely herein lies the strength of revolutionary film art. However, we should not confine ourselves to this. We should give consciousness and organization to the urge which people feel while seeing such masterpieces. We should see to it that people regard these masterpieces as a textbook for their revolutionization, as a weapon for struggle, and bring about new innovations in their lives and practical activities."

The dear leader continued: "Today our working people are effecting great changes in their spirit and morality and attaining a high cultural level. If we conduct organizational and political work purposefully on the strength of such immortal classics as *Sea of Blood* and *The Flower Girl*, we will be able to promote the three revolutions more vigorously. The *Minju Choson* should be the first to try this, which, then, would call forth a great response."

The idea of massive organizational work to put into effect what people learnt from literary and art works was a unique proposition never known in the history of literature and art and the press.

The journalists who had accepted this new proposal of the dear leader with admiration and excitement, lost no time to form an on-the-spot editorial group and rushed to the Anju Coal Mine.

They went into a pit where they operated rock drills, working side by side with colliers, and at breaks organized film shows and popularized film songs.

Seeing the films the miners recalled the wretched life their parents and themselves had experienced before, and bore in mind the revolutionary faith and the will of our people who had fought on stubbornly in defiance of the sea of blood, withstanding all sorts of pain and sorrow while looking up at the great leader. They made firm resolves to fight on vigorously like the heroes of the revolutionary film *Sea of Blood*, adapted from the immortal classic of the same title written during the anti-Japanese revolutionary struggle, regarding the film as a textbook for revolutionization and as a weapon in struggle.

They lighted the first signal-fire in forming the "Pibada" (sea of blood—Tr.) guards in the pit to embody in practice their fervent aspiration to live and work like the heroes in the film.

On the night of January 11, 1973, the dear leader examined the editorial plan of the *Minju Choson* for the special issue woven with such impressive news, and gave meticulous guidance to the titles, contents and edition of articles. Under his great plan and scrupulous care, the "Pibada" guards were created and the news was made public through the January 13, 1973 issue.

Seeing this issue he was pleased more than anyone else. He said that since the guards of the working class had taken the first grand step forward, agricultural workers should follow suit. After this he again dispatched the *Minju Choson* journalists to the socialist cooperative fields.

According to his instructions that in the countryside they

had better learn from the revolutionary film *The Flower Girl*, the newspaper organized an editorial group and sent it to the farmers in Mundok County. There the group energetically carried out its assignment just as the anti-Japanese guerrillas did.

Thus the "Ggotpanunchonyo" (the flower girl—Tr.) guards came into being in that county. This fact was made known all over the country through the January 23 issue of the *Minju Choson*.

These two guards which had been created on his proposal and under his energetic guidance, accelerated the cause for modelling the whole society on the Juche idea, making new innovations and great strides on the fronts of industry and agriculture.

Meanwhile, the journalists submitted to him a photographic album showing the struggle of guardsmen, the working people's opinions about the organization of the guards, and the special issues for guardsmen. After checking them, he instructed in concrete terms that the propaganda of the guards and the edition of the newspaper should be improved to meet the purpose.

When the torches lighted in Anju and Mundok Counties spread all over the country, the dear leader showed great interest in them and saw to it that the guardsmen played the role of shock brigade in socialist construction, and carefully guided the edition of the newspaper to fulfil its purpose.

He sent the journalists to the Kim Chaek Iron Works which was struggling on the main front of grand socialist construction, to help the "Pibada" guardsmen take the lead in creating a new speed in the expansion project of the iron works. He also guided the "Ggotpanunchonyo" guardsmen to be frontrankers in making innovations to reach the Six-Year Plan target for grain production.

Indeed, the struggle to emulate the heroes of the immortal classics proposed and led by the dear leader, displayed great vitality and contributed richly to inspiring our people to fresh innovations and rapid progress.

Intensive Telecast of *Song of Comradeship*

The dear leader spoke highly of *Song of Comradeship*, the theme song of the Korean feature film *Star of Korea* and instructed that the song should be broadcast and telecast more often.

One day in the middle of December 1980, the dear leader called an official and expressed his satisfaction with the good presentation of *Song of Comradeship* on the radio and TV. He said:

"**The *Song of Comradeship* must be repeated on the radio and TV just as it is done now.**"

This was a meaningful statement that he made after correctly catching the profound idea contained in the song. It is a song that gives a real presentation of the loftiest comradely affection and revolutionary ethics with which in the late 1920s and the early 1930s—the dawn of the Korean revolution—the young communists of Korea defended the great leader with all devotion, holding him in high esteem as the lodestar of the Korean revolution and as the pivot of unity, out of the revolutionary faith and lofty ethics they had found in the struggle.

The dear leader had this song broadcast and telecast continually and extensively. He did this with a high aim to train our people and particularly the new generation into the dependable revolutionary vanguards carrying forward, not only today but even in the distant future, the glorious tradition of the young communists who in the past had defended the headquarters of our revolution even in the harsh ordeals they had endured under the guidance of the great leader.

After he gave his first instructions to popularize this song, the telecasters devoted all their thoughts and energies and in a short time succeeded in adapting it to the TV at a high ideological and artistic level.

Drawing on their valuable experience in this success, they then bent down to the job of making a TV version of *I'll Be the Flower to Herald the Spring*, theme song of the feature film *The Fourteenth Winter* which portrayed an unassuming heroine, a song which had been already broadcast.

As a consequence, these two songs were broadcast both by the radio and TV, causing a great sensation among the listeners and viewers, mainly because they were of high ideological and artistic value and also were presented continually and intensively.

Shortly before the *Song of Comradeship* was televized, the song *I'll Be the Flower to Herald the Spring* was diffused through the radio. At the outset, it was broadcast several times a day for a good period, according to the instructions of the dear leader. But, gradually it was sent on the air twice a day, because they thought it was enough. As a result, it became hardly noticeable on a day's programme when the song was broadcast.

One day the dear leader who had known this fact told the officials that their enthusiasm should not cool down with the lapse of time, and induced them to send the song repeatedly.

In keeping with his instructions, the *Song of Comradeship* and *I'll Be the Flower to Herald the Spring* were radiocast and telecast in turn several times every day.

This was really an exceptional way of drawing up the intensive programme that added a new page to the TV history.

Even after creating this new form of intensive TV broadcasting, the dear leader reemphasized the need to telecast these two songs continually.

This is why these songs are continually broadcast through radio and TV even today. Listening to them, our working people and younger generation are inspired with a fervent desire to live like the young communists who were loyal to the great leader at the dawn of the Korean revolution, as well as the unassuming heroes of today.

PERSONALLY STANDING IN THE FOREFRONT

During the Sixth Congress of the Workers' Party of Korea

On September 16, 1980 when the historic Sixth Congress of the Workers' Party of Korea and its 35th founding anniversary were near at hand, the dear leader Comrade Kim Jong Il, who always organizes all work in a foresighted way and directs it at the head, called in an official in charge of the Party paper to ensure that highlights were given to the news of the Sixth Party Congress and the celebrations of the Party's 35th anniversary.

The dear leader analysed the shortcomings revealed previously in the edition of the newspaper concerning Party congresses, with a high degree of political keenness and extraordinary insight. Drawing on this lesson, he instructed that it was important to report well the opening and closing sessions of the Sixth Party Congress. Then he gave the official a task of making a detailed editorial plan for the newspaper during the Party Congress.

The Sixth Party Congress and the celebrations of the Party's 35th anniversary were great political events unique in their character, scale and significance.

The Party paper *Rodong Sinmun*, therefore, should have mapped out a plan well in advance to drastically increase the pages and tackle an enormous amount of reports so as to give prominence to these great events every day.

The officials of the newspaper, however, were sluggish and did not make a proper plan of reports, on the plea that there was nearly a month ahead of the Party Congress.

Just at this time the dear leader made a deeper study of how to edit reports on the Party Congress than anyone else, and gave wise instructions, mapping out a new plan without sticking to the precedent and designing everything ambitiously.

The Party paper editors who found the clear direction and gained confidence from the dear leader's valuable teachings for the first time, hurried to make a plan for editing reports on the Sixth Party Congress.

On October 8, two days before the opening of the Party Congress, the dear leader took time to examine the editorial plan from his tight schedule for taking care of the whole work related to the Party Congress and the celebrations of the Party's 35th founding anniversary. That day he examined as many as 101 pages (80 pages of the layout and 21 pages of typesetting composition) and gave detailed instructions on editing the newspaper ambitiously and in a fresh and neat way, and at an incomparably higher political level than at the time of previous Party congresses or important political functions.

Particularly, the dear leader scrupulously guided the layout for the October 11 issue of the newspaper which was to report the opening session of the Party Congress. That day he examined one by one the four plans prepared by the Party paper. He chose the first plan and revised the vertical banner headline on the first page into *The Sixth Congress of the Workers' Party of Korea Opens* and told the people concerned to make the title formal.

The dear leader also examined the two plans of the typesetting composition for the October 11 issue. The first plan was to edit the picture of the great leader on the platform in the full-length on the first page beside the vertical banner headline. He marked off a circle on this spot expressing his concurrence. The second page set up the text of the opening address in No. 5 type. He wrote the number "6", indicating that a smaller type should be used. And on the third page which set up the text of the report in No. 5 type, he also wrote the number "5" showing that the report should be edited in a bigger type than the opening address.

The dear leader scrupulously examined the layout of the paper which was to report the opening session of the Party Congress to every letter and every line, and corrected the shortcomings. He then pointed out:

"I've examined the editorial plan of the newspaper to be issued during the Party Congress. It is advisable to give a vertical red-coloured headline *The Sixth Congress of the Workers' Party of Korea Opens* **on the first page. A big photograph of the leader on the platform should be printed at the top on the first page. The picture of his reading the report should be edited on the third page and the photo of the platform should be moved to the second page. You should use No. 6 type for the opening address and No. 5 type for the report."**

Working on the Party paper well past midnight both on October 10, the opening day of the Sixth Party Congress, and October 11, the dear leader explained to the Party paper editors in detail how to allocate the space for the articles and photos. This enabled the newsmen to edit the day's major functions correctly irrespective of the precedent in conformity with their political importance. And on October 13, he closely studied the newspaper page after page not in his office but in the meeting hall, thus leading the staff to edit it purposefully.

Furthermore, the dear leader attached great importance to the edition of reports on foreign delegations and scrupulously guided the editorial staff to do it on an unprecedentedly big scale. The historic Sixth Congress of our Party and the celebrations of its 35th anniversary were grand international festivals. They were attended by 177 foreign delegations from 118 countries of the five continents, including those led by party and state heads. He paid deep attention to the report on the activities of foreign delegations, who were to participate in the Party Congress and the anniversary celebrations, and particularly on the great leader's activities with them. And already on September 27, prior to the opening of the Party Congress, he gave detailed instructions on handling well the news of the foreign delegations from their arrival till their departure.

As a result, the newspaper could daily carry reports on the foreign delegations on a high politico-ideological level and on an unprecedentedly large scale.

As seen above, in those historic days when the Sixth Party Congress and the celebrations of its 35th anniversary were held, the *Rodong Sinmun* brought about a new revolutionary change not only in the scale of its publication but also in its political level and theoretical depth as well as in its editing process such as the form and method of layout, the writing of articles, camera work and photo production, and typesetting and printing, and managed to play its proper role worthy of the Party organ. All this is attributable to the dear leader's direct guidance to its editorial work.

On the Eve of the Celebration Meeting

The following is a story about what took place on September 8, 1978, the eve of the celebration meeting of the 30th founding anniversary of the Democratic People's Republic of Korea.

Late at night, the dear leader paid a second visit to the Pyongyang Indoor Stadium, the venue of the meeting. He attentively looked awhile at the spacious and magnificent hall. Everything in the meeting place was associated with his deep care. The portrait of the great leader decorated with fragrant flowers, the background of the platform symbolic of the 30th anniversary of the Republic, and the rows of desks and chairs resembling columns of soldiers on parade.

With a look of great satisfaction, the dear leader repeated that the meeting place was well arranged. Then he looked at the platform and the seats for the guests upstairs, saying that it was indeed nice to see that the ladders for camera shot were withdrawn from the front of the platform, and the TV cameras were moved to the seats for the guests upstairs. In fact, in the forenoon there were many ladders for TV, documentary and photo shooting in front of the platform according to the established practice for news coverage.

The dear leader who came to the meeting place in the morning, was lost in deep thought awhile as his eyes reached them. Then he told the officials in a grave tone that the ladders prevented the platform with the great leader from being clearly visible and the participants of the meeting from seeing the leader. And he said that they had better take away all of the ladders and put the TV cameras upstairs.

As soon as they had followed his instructions the front of the platform became clearer and the hall looked brighter.

After expressing his great pleasure with the open platform, the dear leader elucidated the principles to be adhered to in the on-the-spot relay. He said:

"In fixing the place of the camera, the cameramen's

first consideration should be how to take the leader's best picture."

Giving a look around at the officials, the dear leader said he would like to see how it was screened, before he strode towards the seats for the guests upstairs. When he reached there the TV broadcasters courteously greeted him. He gave a warm handshake as he mounted on the camera stand and adjusting the camera, looked at the platform and the rostrum.

The dear leader was closely watching the viewfinder to select the brightest and best picture and frame. This thrilling scene was expressive of a beautiful blossom that has come into bloom thanks to his intense loyalty—his desire to have the great leader most respectfully on the high platform of the celebration meeting as the entire people wished, the leader who illumined the road ahead of the era with the brilliant rays of the Juche idea and brought a new spring of liberation to this land and built a prosperous socialist Korea in a matter of 30 years under the banner of the Republic.

The eve of the red-letter day was wearing on. But the dear leader was adjusting the camera putting all his energies into his work. Soon he turned his gaze off the camera and told the cameraman to fix it in that position, saying that now everything was clearly visible.

The platform was seen very clearly through the viewfinder and the frame was selected in a most ideal way. This complete screen was not merely a product of the shooting tools. This perfection of photo technique was a fruit of the dear leader's unboundedly pure loyalty which was turned into the lines, colours and light.

The dear leader could not feel at rest even after he had personally selected an excellent picture frame, and now he paid more attention to the background which nobody had, until then, given any consideration.

He pointed out one shortcoming after another, which appeared in the background of the great leader's picture, and taught in detail how to correct them.

The officials were gripped by a solemn sentiment as they watched the impressive scene when the dear leader was trying to get a perfect screen without taking off his eyes from the viewfinder.

The dear leader gave a look around at the officials and said with great satisfaction before he left the indoor stadium: **"It's all right now. If you relay the scene regulating the screen skilfully, you will be able to get a picture of the leader respectfully on the TV screen."**

The bright Orion's Belt over the nocturnal sky had by now almost disappeared behind the horizon, and the gala day was dawning.

This Is How the TV Broadcast Started

The General TV Department of the Radio and TV Broadcasting Committee has a legend-like story. This is a story about how the first trial transmission of TV broadcasting was conducted over 20 years ago.

Early in 1961 the broadcasting workers organized a group for the production of equipment involving a few technicians, and started to study technical documents and make designs with a view to begin TV broadcasting.

In those days, however, there was not a single technician who had worked before in TV and so experience was lacking. There were no equipment and materials. So they failed to make any success worth mentioning, though six months had passed since they started work.

Just around this time the dear leader visited them,

showing them in detail the orientation and the ways and means to tackle it, and also inspiring them with confidence.

One month later, on the afternoon of a clear July day, he again called to see them.

When he was told that after strenuous inquiry the equipment production group had succeeded in screening objects with the TV facilities which they had manufactured themselves, the dear leader postponed everything and came to the Radio and TV Broadcasting Committee. As soon as he arrived there, he made for the work place of the equipment production group.

The group members were silently standing ill at ease and were at a loss what to do, for they met him in a room littered with equipment. But he squeezed everyone's hand and congratulated them on their first success, smiling.

They started moving the cameras in their desire to show him a good picture as soon as possible. However, no matter how much they changed the position of the cameras, all the pictures were dim and their clearness did not improve.

The dear leader watched the group members hurrying with their work with vexation. After a while of thinking, he asked them whether they had inquired into the reason for the dimness of the pictures. When he saw them hesitating unable to give any answer, he pointed out that the question of the lenses should be solved above all to make the screen clear, and then he told them:

"You are now doing an honourable job to realize the leader's far-reaching plan to set up TV broadcast in our country as soon as possible....

"I'll do my level best to help your work."

The dear leader regarded himself as a member of the group for production of TV facilities and made great efforts to complete the work.

When the TV staff succeeded in securing images with the

object lens he himself had given them, the dear leader shared their joy and inspired them with confidence to finish the production of TV equipment.

Sometimes he sat with the group members discussing technical problems arising in the production of video transmitters and audio transmitters and explaining to them detailed ways for their solution.

A few days prior to the 30th anniversary of the founding of the Korean People's Army, he proposed them to have a try at on-the-spot relay and minutely told them about technical problems that might crop up in relay broadcasting.

On April 23, 1962 the broadcasting workers unexpectedly met the dear leader at Kim Il Sung Square. At that time they were taking a trial shot of the parade of the Worker-Peasant Red Guards who were having an exercise with the founding anniversary of the Korean People's Army close at hand. They greeted him courteously.

The dear leader gladly received their greetings and appreciated the trouble they had taken in preparing for the on-the-spot relay broadcasting when everything was in short supply. Then he attentively looked at the square appearing on the screen and said the screen was all right, and asked why it was vibrating.

A broadcasting worker replied that it was due to unsatisfactory adjustment. Hearing this, the dear leader said that they should show a clear and stabilized screen to the great leader, and chose for them a site to set up the relay antenna. Besides, he personally adjusted the location of the camera and fixed the best position that would enable them to obtain a stabilized screen. Still not relieved, he said that they should successfully ensure the trial on-the-spot relay broadcast since it was the first of its kind in our country, and warmly shook everyone's hand.

Thanks to the dear leader's energetic guidance they

succeeded in relaying on the spot the Pyongyang city mass rally celebrating the historic 30th anniversary of the Korean People's Army, and thus gave great joy to the great leader.

This was a precious fruition brought about by the energetic guidance, unremitting efforts and great favours of the dear leader who had always solved difficult technical problems and elucidated concrete orientation and ways since the production of TV equipment started.

This made it possible to declare to the whole world the birth of the Korean Central TV Broadcast on March 3, 1963, only two years after the first step was taken towards the production of TV facilities.

Counting the Korean Pepper Bushes with a Journalist

In August 1962, after the historic Changsong Joint Conference of Local Party and Economic Functionaries, the great leader Comrade Kim Il Sung who was giving on-the-spot guidance to many counties in North Pyongan Province in order to improve the living standard of mountainous people, came to Sakju County to guide its Party committee's enlarged plenary meeting.

At the meeting he stressed the need to increase grain production and develop sideline activities including stockbreeding to improve the livelihood of mountain folk, and acquainted himself with farming and stockbreeding conditions in the county through responsible functionaries. He asked them about the acreage of oil-bearing trees the county had created and what kind of trees they were.

Some functionaries gave the figures. After examining them one by one, the great leader said that they were not accurate from a scientific point of view. Then he added: "We should inquire into this matter ourselves."

The dear leader who had been listening to the great leader together with the attendants of the meeting, was lost in deep meditation.

Immediately afterwards they had an interval. A journalist of the Central News Agency who was covering the meeting, was going out towards the vestibule. The dear leader who had been talking to an official called him to his side and asked him if he knew the whereabouts of the Korean pepper bushes.

When the journalist answered in the affirmative, the dear leader asked whether the former had ever reported about the oil-bearing trees in that area. The journalist could not say anything and only bowed his head.

"**Seeing is believing,**" the dear leader said with a slight smile. "**You, the journalist of the Central News Agency, had also better go and see them. Only then will you be able to report them correctly.**"

With these words he was going to start for the pepper bushes without minding the rugged road. When the journalist came out of the entrance accompanying the dear leader, the sky was cloudy and the rain was about to start coming down.

When an official suggested that the dear leader should start when the weather became clear, the leader looked at the approaching dark clouds for a while before he said in a soft yet serious tone:

"**It is a task assigned by the great leader. We must not delay it because of the rain.**"

At the moment the journalist and the official were so moved that they could not say anything more.

The dear leader left for the forest of pepper bushes together with the journalist. The car carrying the dear leader reached the ravine which he had in mind, crossing the neck of the rapids that had suddenly risen.

The pepper bushes were spreading along the ridges on both sides of the ravine. But they did not occupy a large area.

The dear leader's expression was gloomy as he was watching them.

After a while he said that they should not merely know about the rough acreage of the forest of the pepper bushes but should find out the exact number of trees and report it to the great leader. He said: **"You count the trees along that ridge. And you, Comrade journalist, go along this side. I'll count those in the midway."** With these words he stepped towards the midway section.

When the journalist counted almost all the trees in his area, the dear leader had already counted all the trees in the most difficult section and was now returning along the slope in charge of the former.

He waited until the journalist finished counting the remaining trees and asked him how many trees there were in his charge. The latter gave him the figure. The dear leader looked all around before he pointed to the pepper bushes standing at the foot and asked if the journalist included them in his figure. The journalist looked towards the direction indicated by the dear leader, but could not give a prompt answer and only cast down his eyes. There were only two trees.

The dear leader added those two trees to the figure he had already put down in his memo. Then he kindly reasoned with the journalist saying that not a single tree should be omitted because the number was to be reported to the great leader.

Then he pointed out, changing the subject: **"Comrade journalist, you must see things on the spot before you write your articles. Otherwise you may talk big."**

At the moment the journalist blushed. Across his mind flashed the bygones when he used to write his articles in his office only after his conversation with the officials.

As a matter of fact, that day, too, until the meeting opened he had intended to write an article about the creation of pepper bushes after his talk with a local official. Yet he gave no thought to taking the trouble of travelling more than sixteen kilometres across the flooded river to visit this rugged place.

The dear leader told the man that he had better not report about the pepper bushes at the moment but introduce them later when more oil-bearing trees would have been planted. Only then did the journalist realize that the dear leader had taken him there not merely as his guide.

The dear leader took the journalist to the pepper bushes, on the trip which was associated with his loyalty and which he made without minding the bad weather and rugged way. In doing so he intended to make the reporter understand with his whole heart what attitude and position the great leader's journalist should take in looking upon the reality and covering the facts, in writing articles and making reports.

Taking the Place of a Reporter

On May Day, 1966, Pyongyang, the revolutionary capital, was animated from early morning on this international holiday of the working class all over the world. A journalist of the Central News Agency was riding in a car along one of its main streets. Out of the window, he could see endless crowds of working people in their holiday best. He was hurrying on his way to a combined-arms military academy of the Korean People's Army upon hearing the news that the great leader Comrade Kim Il Sung was giving on-the-spot guidance to it.

When the high-speed car was nearing the academy, shouts of cheers burst out in the school grounds and flowery balloons were soaring up into the sky.

No sooner had the car reached the entrance to the academy than the journalist alighted and elbowed his way through the large crowd. But the great leader had already entered the academy building. So he was very much flurried: he had failed to cover the scene of the enthusiastic welcome accorded by the teaching staff and cadets to the great leader. The more he thought of this, the more he felt vexed.

Just at this moment the dear leader Comrade Kim Jong Il, whom he had respected heartily, beckoned him at the entrance to the academy, calling: **"Come here, please, Comrade journalist."**

Overjoyed and full of emotion, the journalist rushed up to him and courteously greeted him. The dear leader gladly met him shaking his hand. Then he asked:

"Have you been told belatedly to cover the news?"

"No," replied the journalist, "I was making preparations after I had been told about it and...." He could say nothing more, and only dropped his head.

The dear leader produced his memo pad, saying that when he had got there he could find no journalists, so he had jotted the welcome scene.

"The dear leader should cover the news, taking the place of a reporter!" At this thought he was filled with strong emotion.

The dear leader told him to write down what he would dictate and opened his memo pad. He read:

"The great leader came to the academy accompanied by members of the Political Committee of the Party Central Committee and other cadres. Welcoming him at the main entrance were the Chief of General Staff of the People's Army and the responsible functionaries of the academy."

Then he gave the names of those members of the Political Committee of the Party Central Committee who were accompanying the great leader and also the names and posts of other members of the suite one by one.

He continued:

"The great leader reviewed the guard of honour and ac-

knowledged the enthusiastic cheers of those who welcomed him.

"**All the soldiers and their family members came out and, waving bouquets, fervently welcomed the leader.**"

As he was putting down in his memo what was dictated by the dear leader, the journalist could see before his eyes the stirring scene when, upon the great leader's arrival, the teaching staff, cadets and the family members of the soldiers began to stamp their feet with flower bundles in their hands, shouting at the top of their voice, "Long live the great leader Comrade Kim Il Sung!" He also seemed to see the fatherly leader who was inspecting the formation of parading soldiers in front of the main entrance, the soldiers with intense loyalty in their hearts, and acknowledging the enthusiastic cheers of those who welcomed him with his hand upraised and with a bright smile on his face.

What the dear leader dictated was not merely data for news coverage but rather a perfect article vividly depicting the scene of welcome. The only thing the journalist had to do was to rewrite on copy papers what the dear leader had told him. Overjoyed at this thought, he looked up to him.

Having dictated everything he had put down in his memo pad, the dear leader pointed out:

"**The great leader is now inspecting the interior of the academy.**

"**You should not make haste but try to collect information well.**"

With these words the dear leader told him to enter the school quickly, and walked ahead. The journalist entered the school building with a throbbing heart and covered the very important instructions the great leader gave while inspecting various research rooms. The leader stressed the need to firmly establish Juche in military education and teach the soldiers tactics conforming to our actual conditions so as to bring all of them to be competent commanders.

At that time the dear leader was near the reporter, looking

at him with benevolent eyes and encouraging him to write down without a single omission what the great leader was saying. Sometimes he looked into the latter's memo, paying close attention to his activities to collect information.

As a result, that day the journalist was able to cover the great leader's on-the-spot guidance in detail and ensure its timely report.

At the Opening Ceremony of the Children's Palace

On September 30, 1963, there was the opening ceremony of the Pyongyang Students and Children's Palace, a comprehensive school for intellectual, moral and physical education and a centre for extracurricular education.

The great leader was to attend the ceremony. The spacious ground in front of the palace was packed to capacity with girls in jackets with multi-coloured sleeves and skirts, and students and citizens with bouquets in their hands who were awaiting his arrival.

The journalists of the newspaper *Minju Chongnyon* (now the newspaper *Rodong Chongnyon* issued by the Kumsong Youth Publishing House) were finishing their preparations to cover the facts in the hall on the first floor of the palace together with those of other press organs.

Just at the moment the dear leader Comrade Kim Jong Il strode to them, his face beaming with a bright smile. When the journalists greeted him, he warmly shook their hands, asking in a gentle voice if they were getting along well. Looking round at them he said that he had just made his rounds of the rooms of the palace, and warmly encouraged them by remarking that they would have to do a great deal of work that day. He continued that the palace built under the care of the great leader was indeed a grand palace for extracurricular education of the students.

"In a little while we shall declare the opening of the palace to the whole world," he said. **"You should report this meaningful event well."**

With these words the dear leader approached the journalists from the *Minju Chongnyon* (Democratic Youth—Tr.). He told them that they should play the role of the master and do a good job in covering the facts that day because the palace was a house for students and children. And he exhorted them to deal with the day's function better than any other newspapers.

Bearing deep in their mind his earnest instructions, the journalists of the *Minju Chongnyon* were making their determination to report the opening ceremony on the highest level.

The great leader arrived at the palace at 7.00 p.m. sharp. Shouts of cheers shook the palace. Lovely girls tied Children's Union's scarf around the great leader's neck and presented him fragrant bouquets. The children competed with each other in grasping the hands of the benevolent father Marshal Kim Il Sung and clinging to his sleeves to get into his embrace. The cameramen and reporters quickly got down to their work lest they should miss this moment.

After a while the great leader entered the palace acknowledging the enthusiastic cheers of the crowd.

Though he was very busy aiding the great leader in his on-the-spot guidance, the dear leader paid close attention to the news coverage of the journalists.

When the great leader moved to another room after his inspection of the automobile study room, the journalists from the *Minju Chongnyon* were still in this room, collecting information through a student who had shown the great leader the driving practice. When they went out of the room, they deeply felt their blunder.

The great leader was already giving very important instructions in the next room. In their confusion, they made haste to enter the room, but they could not because there were many suite members. So they were left stranded.

The dear leader saw their uneasiness and asked the entourage to make room for them. And only when the great leader was leaving for another room did the dear leader ask the journalists why they were late, remarking: "**You seem to go into detail when collecting the materials. That's a good thing. But you should not leave the great leader when you cover functions held in his presence. Only then will you be able to impressively cover his on-the-spot guidance, and also write good articles. You will be quite able to enrich the news coverage better after this function is over.**"

The journalists were greatly moved as they were listening to the dear leader who detailed the methods of covering the functions held in the great leader's presence.

While inspecting various study rooms and practice rooms of the palace, the great leader instilled high hope for the future in the students and children and encouraged them to have a fervent spirit of inquiry. Then he got to the observation platform on the tower.

The cameramen quickened their steps competing with each other to take a good picture of the great leader on the tower.

After watching them awhile with affectionate eyes, the dear leader appreciated their efforts, saying: "**Whenever we have functions, I see the cameramen doing a tough job. They are busy even without a short respite. This is because pictures should be taken in the opportune moment unlike writing articles.**" Saying this he looked affectionately at the journalists.

Soon he came up to the lift and explained that the lift had been made by our working class in response to the great leader's instructions. Then he told the moving story associated with it and said that they should introduce this material in their article.

Now it was time for the dear leader to take the lift. There were many officials to whom priority should have been given in using the lift. But the dear leader gave precedence to the journalists as he joined them. It was already dark outside when they got to the observation platform accompanying the dear leader.

Watching the brilliantly illuminated splendid scene of Pyongyang, the great leader gave detailed instructions on many questions including that of building up the observation platform and improving its management.

After his inspection of all the rooms and facilities, the great leader headed for a lounge late in the evening. The journalists hurried there to receive his instructions. But the room was not large enough and their entrance was limited.

Just at this moment the dear leader came there and acquainted himself with how the matter stood. Then he looked at the journalists for a while and said: **"You comrade journalists from the *Minju Chongnyon* are also here.... The room seems narrow."** Then he addressed the officials:

"These comrades should be let in. They must immediately write an article which is to be issued tomorrow. How can they write the report on the opening ceremony without receiving the leader's instructions?

"Let's allow them in, even though the room is narrow."

Thanks to him, that day the journalists had the honour of receiving the great leader's instructions.

The great leader clearly indicated the road to be followed by the students and children's palace as a centre for extracurricular education and showed deep concern for building up the palace better and improving its management. Then he said before he rose from his seat: **"The children are the kings in our country."**

The journalists thought to themselves: This precisely

should be the kernel of our article! Thanks to the fatherly leader's solicitude the palace has been erected today and the children have become the kings of the country and are growing up envying nothing in this world. We should boast of this reality loudly!

Remembering the dear leader's words, the journalists could picture in their minds what they were going to write.

Thanks to the dear leader's profound solicitude, next day the *Minju Chongnyon* managed to give large space to the report on the opening ceremony of the students and children's palace with a picture of the benevolent great leader. This immensely delighted the young students throughout the country.

On the Site of Video-tape Recording

On April 10, 1969, the dear leader Comrade Kim Jong Il called in the TV technicians and editorial staff of the Radio and TV Broadcasting Committee of the Democratic People's Republic of Korea and gave them his video-tape recorder, telling them to record the performance of the cinema artists being held at the Pyongyang Grand Theatre at that time.

Greatly moved, the broadcasting workers hurried to the theatre even without having expressed their gratitude to him properly. They pushed ahead with preparations for video-tape recording, fixing the location of cameras and setting up illuminators.

When their preparations were nearing the end, the dear leader came to them.

"He has spent so much time to teach us recording techniques, and is now even coming here...." At this thought the broadcasting workers felt high respect for the dear leader who attached great importance to TV broadcasting and was constantly giving them meticulous guidance in spite of the heavy pressure of the task of leading the revolution and construction.

Greatly delighted at the fact that they were to record in the presence of the dear leader, the TV workers reexamined the technical conditions of all their equipment in detail. Then they told him that everything was ready.

The dear leader said with satisfaction: **"Let's start recording."**

The curtain rose and the recording of the first piece started. Everything was going on smoothly. But soon the dear leader who had been closely watching the screen, wore a gloomy expression. Seeing this, the officials felt ill at ease. The dear leader who had been attentively looking into the screen for a good while with a worried look, asked why it was not clear. The officials had not paid attention to the clearness of the screen so they could not answer him promptly.

Seeing this, the dear leader acquainted himself with various technical problems before he said that the feeble lighting seemed to be the cause. And he immediately called the officials concerned and told them to provide brighter lamps.

Before long the stage became much brighter than before, and so did the screen.

"Now, it's all right," said the dear leader with satisfaction, and referred to the method of selecting pictures:

"Unlike the cinema, the TV has a small screen. Therefore, you should close up the object, and should not make it small. In particular, this is all the more so when you show men.

"Only then will one take interest in looking into the TV screen."

The hearts of the broadcast workers were throbbing with great excitement as they were listening to what the dear leader said. Basing himself on a profound analysis of the specific features of the TV and cinema, he indicated a very important guiding principle to be adhered to in projecting TV images and directing the screen.

They strove to close up objects in projecting and managed to get good pictures.

During the whole period of video-tape recording the dear leader came to the theatre almost every day. When the recording of one piece was over, he reviewed the video-tape, pointing to every merit and shortcoming and personally showing them how to record stage pieces and what level the recording should reach. When he saw the screen vibration, he told them to eliminate such a phenomenon because it might tire the eyes of the people.

Following the recording at the Grand Theatre, the dear leader got the TV workers to record an acrobatic performance and then athletic sports. He organized a football game between the best teams for their video-tape recording and again came to the site of recording. When the work was over, he played back the video-tape, pointing to the shortcomings, and praised them more than they deserved:

"Now the screen is clear. Both direction and projecting are good. In this way you'll be able to develop the videocast."

Like this the dear leader came to the work site of the broadcasting staff and guided them, teaching them everything. Thanks to his energetic and meticulous guidance, the proud history of the videocast was progressing.

To Ensure Promptness of Information

One day in early August 1962, it started raining from early morning. By midday it was pouring in sheets sending up misty spray. To make the matter worse, the wind was blowing and there were thunderbolts.

As he was watching the rainstorm through the window, a journalist from the Korean Central News Agency felt strong uneasiness. When he returned to his lodging after radioing to his news agency the pictures of the scenes of the historic Changsong joint conference, he was told to send other ones because the pictures were not clear.

"Shall I transmit again?" he thought to himself. He knew too well that in such a bad weather picture transmission could not be successful.

When he was at a loss what to do there was another phone from his news agency urging him to radio the pictures again. He wished he could fly to Pyongyang if he had wings.

Just at this moment, an official unexpectedly conveyed him a glad news that the dear leader Comrade Kim Jong Il wanted to see him.

The overjoyed journalist hurried to the dear leader who gladly met him and asked:

"Comrade journalist, have you transmitted the pictures related to the Changsong joint conference held in the great leader's presence?"

"Yes..." said the journalist, but he could not conclude because he felt guilty of his failure to radio pictures properly.

The dear leader already saw through his feelings and said in a softer voice: **"You mean you've radioed them but they ask for other ones?"**

Hearing the journalist's reply, the dear leader said that the man should have let him know about the circumstances and continued:

"You should not delay even for a moment the reports related to functions held in the leader's presence....

"The leader's picture should be clear and should not have even a trivial flaw. You should display a high degree of loyalty in handling the leader's picture."

After a while the dear leader asked how they could radio

pictures better. He heard the journalist's opinion and then said:

"**You should leave for Pyongyang quickly with the photos relating to today's function. Photo transmission may not be successful because it is lightening now.**

"**I'll provide a car. You should thoroughly defend the leader's picture lest it should be spoilt even a little.**"

Listening to him, the journalist could not say anything because he was moved beyond description. Some time ago, early in the morning when the mist had not yet cleared off, the dear leader came to the meeting place and personally chose the location for camera shot in order to take a better picture of the great leader who was to guide the historic meeting. And now he was so much concerned and showing great solicitude for a smooth transmission of the photos.

When the journalist was trying to calm down his emotion, the dear leader called an official and told him to get a car ready. Then he asked him about the road leading to Pyongyang. He seemed not to feel at ease even after he heard the reply; he listened to the sound of the rain and wind. Then he called on the phone the officials in those localities through which the car was to pass, and asked them in detail how much the rivers had risen and whether the bridges were safe or not.

Then he once again told the journalist that he should not delay even a moment in reporting the historic meeting held in the leader's presence, and rose from his seat with the words: "**Let's go to the car.**" When the journalist told him that the storm was vehement, the dear leader said that he would feel at rest only when he saw him leaving, and walked ahead.

A car was already waiting in front of the vestibule. It was the dear leader's car.

"**Get on the car quickly. The rain seems to be continuing for it's the wet season. So you must be careful on your way.**"

His infinitely gentle voice expressed the very love of the parents who see off their children leaving for a long journey.

But the journalist could not get on the car. He saw the mercilessly sprinkling rain drops soaking the dear leader's clothes.

The dear leader said, pushing his back lightly: **"I'm all right. I trouble myself about how you'll go through this rain. Don't worry about me, and leave quickly."**

The journalist was moved so much that he could not even bow properly to the dear leader. Seeing him the dear leader said he was afraid that he might catch a cold, he again urged him to get on the car.

The journalist wished that his whole body could be the blue sky so as to protect the dear leader from the rain. But he could not even provide him an umbrella before he got into the car. And now he could hardly leave the place.

"Don't worry about me, but leave quickly," the dear leader said in a soft voice, looking at the journalist with affectionate eyes. **"I'll be waiting for the report."**

Before long the car left. Now it was pouring down more heavily. However, the warm rays of the sun were penetrating into the heart of the journalist riding along the road of love and glory opened by the dear leader himself.

Thanks to such profound care of the dear leader the *Rodong Sinmun* and other newspapers could carry on the following morning the picture of the great leader guiding the historic Changsong Joint Conference of Local Party and Economic Functionaries.

ENERGETIC AND METICULOUS GUIDANCE

The First Stereophoto of the Great Leader

In early June of 1972, a cameraman of the Korean Central News Agency happened to receive a happy news.

Having long arranged a colour stereophoto centre out of an ardent wish to take an image of the respected leader Comrade Kim Il Sung in the stereophoto, the dear leader Comrade Kim Jong Il summoned the cameraman.

Taking a car sent by the dear leader, the cameraman was deeply moved. No sooner had he arrived at Samjiyon, a historic place, than he hurried to the dear leader to greet him and get instructions from him.

At that time the dear leader was staying there, giving on-the-spot guidance in Ryanggang Province. The cameraman made a polite bow to him. The dear leader returned the greeting, thanked him for coming all the way, and then asked him about preparations for the photograph and instructed him to be well prepared to take pictures successfully.

"Our people will be very happy to see the image of the great leader standing by Lake Samji," the dear leader said. **"Tomorrow morning you should take a colour stereophoto of the great leader by Lake Samji against the background of Mt. Paekdu."**

He then encouraged the cameraman to have a good rest that day and take a good picture with a refreshed spirit next morning.

Going back to his room, the cameraman could not rest. Looking outside through the window he thought deeply of his important duty, when he saw the dear leader walking along the lakeside.

He made his way through the woods full of flowers and climbed up on an elevated land, clutching twigs. Deep in meditation, he looked at the snow-covered Mt. Paekdu for a while, and then slowly walked along a lane between white ashes.

The cameraman thought that the dear leader was passing the time away, enjoying the beautiful landscape of Lake Samji.

Some time later, an official came in and informed the cameraman that the dear leader had personally chosen the spot where the photo of the fatherly leader was to be taken next morning. The cameraman went out of the room, following the official. He arrived at the spot and looked round the landscape.

Two gently swaying white birches which seemed to tell of the unforgettable story about the great General Kim Il Sung who had made a historic march into the homeland, breaking through the enemy's strict cordon in May 1939 during the heroic anti-Japanese armed struggle and instilled confidence in victory in the minds of his soldiers who were drinking clear water in Lake Samji; the clear lake mirroring the vast stretch of forests; and the faraway majestic Mt. Paekdu with its perpetual snow-capped peak. A mere glance at it warranted many thoughts. It was a magnificent picture, indeed.

The cameraman who was looking in deep thought at the beauty of nature for a long while, felt a burning desire all of a sudden to take a photo of the great leader Comrade Kim Il Sung together with the dear leader Comrade Kim Jong Il in that place of honour.

That night, however, the dear leader went to Hyesan where a function to commemorate the victory day of

Pochonbo battle was taking place.

The cameraman returned to his lodgings, sorry for his unfulfilled hope. The night far advanced and silence reigned all round, but he could not fall asleep.

A knock sounded on the door. An official came in and told him that the dear leader who went to Hyesan just a while before, rang up and said that 10 o'clock in the morning was the best hour for taking a picture by Lake Samji and that at the same hour the next day, a bright image of the fatherly leader should be photographed carefully.

The dear leader personally selected the best site and time for taking a photo, in order to add lustre to the glorious revolutionary history and the immortal revolutionary achievements of the great leader even through a single picture! Indeed, unfathomable is his loyalty towards the great leader.

The glorious dawn set in when the great leader would pose for the photograph at the historic place.

The Paekdu forest swayed endlessly as if welcoming the great leader, the anti-Japanese legendary hero and ever-victorious, iron-willed brilliant commander.

The great leader standing by the memorable Lake Samji with his coat fluttering in the gentle breeze!

The respected leader cast his radiant eyes over the distant mountains as if shaping a brighter future of our revolution which started on Mt. Paekdu.

The first colour stereophoto of the great leader which our people regard with high respect and deep emotions today, was made public thanks to the meticulous guidance and care of the dear leader.

For an Editorial of Great Weight

On February 8, 1973, the dear leader gave important

instructions after reading the first proof of an editorial for the newspaper *Minju Choson* entitled: *Our Revolutionary Film Art Is a Powerful Ideological Weapon for Educating People, Remoulding Their Idea and Developing Society*. At this news all the staff of the newspaper could not suppress their surging emotions.

Vigorous movements of "Pibada" guards and "Ggotpanunchonyo" guards which were started by the dear leader, were taking place in all parts of our country at that time. Our people regarded immortal classics created and popularized in the days of glorious anti-Japanese revolutionary struggle as a textbook of life, a weapon for struggle, and strove to emulate the heroes and heroines of these masterpieces. It was, therefore, of great importance to publish many articles including editorials which would demonstrate the might of revolutionary films such as *Sea of Blood* and *The Flower Girl* based on the immortal classic plays of the same titles.

However, even the *Minju Choson* which was the first to introduce the report on the guards movement in those days, was insensitive to the demand of the times, paying little attention to it.

Fully aware of such a situation, the dear leader brought this shortcoming to the attention of the newspaper's staff and advised them to carry an editorial on the subject of revolutionary films.

Acting on his instructions, the journalists soon bent down to the task. A few days later, on January 31, they completed it. An official reported this to the dear leader, who thanked him for the endeavour and said he would find time to read it as soon as possible. On February 5, he met the leading official and told him that he was then going over the editorial regarding revolutionary films.

The official felt deep gratitude to the dear leader for his meticulous care and guidance shown to the editorial.

A few days after, the dear leader again called the man to his side and pointed out that the introduction to the editorial was too long. He instructed that the first five paragraphs should be shortened into one sentence by referring to the present circumstances in which the whole country was implementing the important tasks given by the great leader at the historic First Session of the Fifth Supreme People's Assembly and in the New Year Address and by mentioning the important place and role of films in this context.

He added that the content of the editorial should be further improved to conform with its title: the title pointed out the importance of films, but the editorial gave too much space to the tradition of film art and its inheritance and development after liberation, making no reference to the specific features of film art, and its great effectiveness in the education of the broad masses.

He continued saying that the major shortcoming in the editorial was that it was written without knowing its readers nor did it arouse government bodies to guarantee material conditions for the spreading of films and properly organize all work with a correct understanding of their functions and role as cultural educators. He also pointed out the shortcomings in sentence construction in detail, and earnestly advised them to discuss and revise the editorial so that it would ensure the unity between the title and content and carry the weight.

The dear leader's instructions opened the eyes of the officials and journalists to the deficiencies of the editorial and the ways to rectify them. Drawing serious lessons from this, they started polishing it with renewed enthusiasm, now correcting its system, now filling up its content and scrutinizing every sentence and word.

He again went over the revised proof, adding finishing touches to the title and content.

Saying that the editorial was now excellent, and pleased with the result, he thanked the journalists.

He spared no pains in making an editorial the best one through his energetic and careful guidance. However, he let the journalists enjoy all the honour for it.

The editorial, a brain child of the dear leader, was carried on the whole front page of the *Minju Choson* dated March 3, 1973. As soon as it was made public, it was acclaimed by the masses, and served as a powerful weapon for inspiring them to live and work like heroes and heroines of the immortal classics.

Three-Colour Ball-Pen Marks

It was while they were editing a special issue for the 62nd anniversary of the great leader Comrade Kim Il Sung's birthday.

The dear leader Comrade Kim Jong Il, in spite of the pressure of the Party and state affairs, went over and over again a political essay, *The Great Juche Era*, written by journalists of the Party paper, until it became perfect.

The writers were deeply moved by the great efforts he had made and the meticulous care he had taken of the political essay, when they saw his benevolent pen marks as they received the first proof he had checked.

Turning over page by page with gratitude, the writers could see at a glance that he had read and revised the essay several times. It was because the paper bore distinctive ball-pen marks of different colours, red, black and blue, which he had left while revising and underlining wherever necessary.

On the first page of the proof he had polished in red and then in black the expression: "because the great leader opened a new epoch and the Party centre upholds his lofty aim."

Similar corrections could also be seen on the next page.

Seeing this, the essayists thought that the dear leader had checked it at least twice. But they could not but be surprised at the last page. He left out one sentence on the last page, with a red ball-pen, and underlined in blue the expression, "the new era of aspirations". So it was evident that the dear leader had read and revised the proof at least three times. When they knew this the essayists were very sorry to have troubled the dear leader again. They were humbled by the art of leadership of the dear leader who was guiding them energetically and meticulously even at the expense of the time for his rest and sleep.

In this way, the dear leader had elaborated on the political essay for the April 15 special issue to commemorate the birthday of the great leader, but he ascribed all merits to the writers.

Till the Finishing Touch Is Given to a Travelogue

On May 14, 1965, a correspondent of the Korean Central News Agency, who had accompanied the great leader Comrade Kim Il Sung on his visit to an Asian country, was summoned by the dear leader Comrade Kim Jong Il when he was preparing a travelogue.

When the correspondent arrived, the dear leader made for the door of his office room and met him cordially.

He thanked the correspondent for coming, saying that he must be tired from continuous efforts after his long journey. He motioned him to sit down and wanted him to talk about his plan for the travelogue.

Fascinated by the personality of the dear leader who was treating him without ceremony as usual, the correspondent explained the plot to him. Then he frankly told him that he was troubled, because of the difficulty in writing the planned article.

Deep in meditation, the dear leader kept silent for a while. He then rose from his seat and strolled about his room, explaining the matters of principle arising in writing a travelogue.

He told the correspondent that as it was a travelogue about the great leader's foreign visit, the article should be somewhat different from the previous ones and that importance should be put on his revolutionary activities.

The correspondent could not help admiring the dear leader who clarified the main point of the travelogue, after grasping the unanimous feelings and aspirations of our people through his unusual intelligence and scientific insight.

He thought, till then, of how to make his travelogue draw the readers' interest and strove mainly to describe foreign elements such as climate and customs in that country. When he realized that he had failed to get rid of outmoded practice of formalism and sticked only to formality and technique, neglecting ideological content, he remained with his head bowed.

Reading the correspondent's mind, the dear leader went on to say in a rather soft voice:

"**If you are to write a good travelogue you should firmly grasp an ideological kernel which you want to emphasize. If you add flesh to the skeleton it will be an excellent travelogue. Success in writing depends on whether the writer grasps the ideological kernel properly or not.**

"**Formality and technique are needed to give a conspicuous description of ideological kernel. Even when you depict a landscape or the way of life, you must never attach importance to itself but subordinate it to the ideological content of an article.**"

Nevertheless, he continued, an article should not be monotonous and stiff but be woven with concrete facts and vivid examples so that the readers could read it with interest.

The correspondent derived a fresh inspiration from the dear leader's teaching. There flashed through his mind subtitles such as *Song of General Kim Il Sung Rings around the Equator*.

The dear leader went out with the correspondent and rode in a car with him through the streets. He told the correspondent that in order to plan a new plot, he should begin in a new style, after some relaxation, and that he should, therefore, ease the strains on his mind and breathe fresh air. Saying this, the dear leader laughed loudly. Winding through the main streets in the city, the car ran along the promenade on the Taedong River lined with drooping willows through which they could see the gently flowing water. In the car the dear leader told him that for a good article the writer should think and think again and prepare himself politically and professionally.

The car arrived at the entrance to the Central News Agency. The dear leader encouraged him to write a good travelogue, while shaking his hand.

The correspondent stood still with a lump in his throat, looking at the car running away.

He wrote passionately one letter after another with a loyal heart.

A few days later, the great leader highly appreciated his travelogue, *Eternal Friendship and Unbreakable Ties*, carried on the press.

"Press the Shutter When You Are Sure of Success"

It was June 24, 1971 when the Sixth Congress of the League of Socialist Working Youth of Korea was in session.

A cameraman of the newspaper *Rodong Chongnyon* went to the congress hall earlier than usual on a mission to report the session.

He checked on his camera again and measured a suitable site for a photo. In this way, he made full preparations for his mission, with a high sense of responsibility, hoping that he would take the great image of the respected leader whom he was anxious to meet anytime.

Some time later, many cameramen came into the hall unexpectedly, each hurried to choose the best place for a photo.

At the very moment, an official came down from the platform and told all cameramen present what the dear leader had just said regarding the taking of photos of the platform, that is, since the League of Socialist Working Youth was master of today's function, the cameraman of the *Rodong Chongnyon* should be given the privilege of holding the best place on the platform.

Accorded such a privilege, the cameraman could not hide his great emotions and joy and firmly resolved to succeed in implementing his honourable duty.

Presently, the dear leader, accompanied by some officials, came to the seats for delegates without formality through a side door.

The cameraman bowed politely to him with a profound feeling of reverence. He acknowledged the cameraman's greeting whom he had met several times in the previous functions held with the participation of the great leader. He then told the cameraman:

"**The great leader will soon appear on the platform. Your paper should be responsible, so you should take excellent photos today. You should photograph in a responsible way the images of the respected leader who will guide the congress work and make a historic speech, so that your newspaper can highlight them and that the pictures can be preserved as precious** historical documents for the education of the rising generation."

Keeping his instructions deep in mind, the cameraman replied politely that he would never fail to discharge his honourable mission admirably.

Looking at the man with trustful eyes, the dear leader asked him where he was to take the photos of the great leader.

The cameraman told him about his plan on different occasions—when the great leader would mount the platform, when he would receive a flower basket and when he would address a speech.

Hearing his answer, the dear leader was satisfied with the spots chosen by the cameraman, and then said:

"You should not approach the great leader too closely when taking his picture, and you should press the shutter only when you are certain that the youth and children would imprint the bright image of the respected leader for ever in their minds."

The dear leader continued to explain the attitude of cameramen towards the photographing of the great leader, as well as the aim of this work, that of making the readers imprint his bright image for ever on their minds. The kind words of the dear leader impressed the cameraman deeply.

Exhorting him to take the photos with great care, the dear leader took his seat modestly on the front row of the seats for the youth delegates.

At nine o'clock sharp, the great leader appeared on the platform amid the enthusiastic cheers.

After a little while, he made the historic speech, "The Youth Must Take Over the Revolution and Carry It Forward."

The cameraman repeatedly took the pictures of the great leader, hoping that he had done his work properly.

As soon as he finished the speech, the youth delegates rose as one applauding and cheering loudly.

At this exciting moment, the cameraman felt the urge to

carry the holy images of the great leader and the dear leader together in the newspaper.

He lost no time to photograph one after another the solemn image of the dear leader who was standing in the centre of the entire audience and at the head of the youth delegates, the successors to the revolution, and cheering the great leader, holding him in great esteem.

The *Rodong Chongnyon* and the *Sonyon Sinmun* dated June 25, 1971, carried the noble image of the great leader who was illuminating the path of the youth movement at the Sixth Congress of the League of Socialist Working Youth and that of the dear leader on the same pages, thus adding lustre to the history of youth and children's publications.

Correcting a Mistake in the Notebook for News Coverage

One day in August 1962, the great leader Comrade Kim Il Sung was giving on-the-spot guidance to the Saenal Cooperative Farm in Sinchon County.

The great leader was surrounded by many officials and farmers. An inexperienced Central News Agency correspondent dared not elbow his way towards him, so he had to cover the news behind the crowd.

At that moment, the dear leader Comrade Kim Jong Il cast affectionate eyes on him wearing a bright smile on his face, and asked him how he could perform his duty as a correspondent accompanying the great leader, standing so far from the scene. He then took the man by the hand and brought him near the great leader.

The correspondent kept back tears of emotion caused by the meticulous care of the dear leader who ensured even the working conditions to which no one paid attention, and enthusiastically wrote down every word of the great leader.

Fine rain drops grew larger and blurred the letters the reporter was writing. He drew his notebook closer to his breast and sheltered it with his head from the rain drops.

Rain drops stopped suddenly. He raised his head to see how it came about. He was surprised to find the smiling dear leader offering him shelter with an umbrella.

Overwhelmed with emotions, the correspondent stood motionless, when the dear leader gesticulated him to carry on with his work.

That day, having looked round the fields, the great leader held a consultative meeting of agricultural workers at the publicity hall of the farm. On this occasion, too, the dear leader made the correspondent sit in the front row, beside him.

The great leader made a very important speech at the meeting, showing the road of agricultural development. The correspondent wrote one word after another in his notebook, with great emotions and excitement.

After the meeting, the dear leader summoned the reporter and told him that he seemed to have misunderstood a certain point in the great leader's teaching, that the leader instructed that "irrigation, electrification, mechanization and chemicalization of agriculture are precisely a communist farming method" and that the reporter was misquoting the expression "communist farming method" for "the way to communism".

As soon as the dear leader indicated the mistake in the notebook, the correspondent read the point once more. Surely, he misquoted the great leader's teaching when he wrote "a communist farming method" as "the way to communism".

If the dear leader had not corrected that mistake right away, the correspondent would have made a big blunder. He was very sorry about this. At the same time, he felt deeply thankful to the dear leader for his kindness and meticulous care shown him to make his news coverage a success. He confirmed his resolution to repay the dear leader's high expectations and confidence with loyalty.

330 Famous Songs

Although this was already a thing of the past, early in the 1970s, many broadcasting workers thought that a broadcast was a means of mass communication and so they neglected music.

It was none other than the dear leader Comrade Kim Jong Il who remedied such an incorrect idea and led them to effect revolutionary changes in the radio service.

Talking to the workers of the Radio and TV Broadcasting Committee on May 29, 1974, the dear leader said:

"**The radio programme should include revolutionary opera music, dynamic songs of grand socialist construction and lyrical songs....**

"**You should not only conduct political propaganda in a big way but also send many songs on the radio to inspire the working people....**

"**You should use narratives only in case of need, and take advantage of music to broadcast the atmosphere of the times.**"

These very important instructions that the radio should use music to reflect the atmosphere of the times and vigorously rouse the working people to the revolution and construction, and that the people should give up the old idea on music and should not take it for an auxiliary but an independent item, one of the major items, in the radio programmes, moved the broadcasting workers to great excitement and an irrepressible sense of self-reproach.

It was not the first time for him to instruct that the radio should deal with music properly.

In December 1973, he sent to the broadcasting workers the musical scores of revolutionary operas including *Sea of Blood* and *The Flower Girl* adapted from the immortal classics of the same titles created in the days of anti-Japanese revolutionary struggle, and hundreds of collections of other songs, instructing that in the broadcast narratives should be properly combined with vigorous revolutionary songs. Later, he instructed them on many occasions to compile musical programmes properly.

Until then, however, the workers failed to understand clearly the intention of the dear leader and devoted a little longer time to music than before, only adjusting broadcasting hours for this purpose.

But instead of reproaching the workers, the dear leader reiterated the need to inspire the spirit of the times by means of music and use narratives only when indispensable, so that new changes were effected in broadcasting work.

In accordance with his instructions, the broadcasting workers made vigorous endeavours to rectify their mistakes with regard to music and to give prominence to it.

Moreover, he said that many famous songs should be broadcasted and made sure that this instruction was implemented.

On July 7, 1974, he personally listened to thousands of songs and selected 330 songs from among them. He then compiled a list of famous songs and sent it to the Radio and TV Broadcasting Committee.

These songs deeply impressed those working in the committee. They were more than grateful to the dear leader for the care and warm love he had shown them in order to introduce revolutionary changes in broadcasting work.

On March 11, 1977, the dear leader again chose 1,177 excellent songs, and, later on, several hundred songs.

Thanks to the energetic and careful guidance of the dear leader, many famous songs have been broadcasted, with the result that the radio programmes as a whole have assumed new colouring and enhanced the revolutionary spirit of the times.

REGARDING A SMALL THING AS IMPORTANT

"The Train Broadcast Is Very Important"

It was March 11, 1975. A cold sleet of early spring was falling from early morning. In spite of such bad weather, the dear leader Comrade Kim Jong Il visited the three-revolution exhibition hall towards noon and dropped in at the train broadcasting studio where no official had ever come.

Looking around the inside of the studio, he spoke highly of its arrangement. He tried a tape recorder and looked carefully at the microphone.

An announcer-curator was standing by the door at a loss what to do. Seeing her, the dear leader who was sitting on a chair putting aside the cushion which was on it, asked her if she was a train announcer, and motioned to a seat beside him, urging her to come in. However, she was hesitant because the studio was too small to pass in front of him. He knew her feeling and stood up, saying, **"Do not hesitate. Come in and try to speak over the radio."** He then took her by the hand and made her sit beside him. And he drew the microphone in a corner of the table near to her, saying that it would be difficult for her to speak, if the microphone was far away.

"Let me hear how fluently you speak," he went on. **"Let me see if you are as good as the announcers of the Radio and TV Broadcasting Committee are. Now, have a try."**

She was embarrassed. Seeing this, he encouraged her to do it with the presence of mind. Only then did she take the courage to begin to speak.

When she finished her long speech, he patted her gently on the shoulder, saying, "**You have done well. Proficient. You are on a high level. That will do.**"

Receiving undeserved words of praise, she did not know what to do. He asked her in detail how long she spoke over the microphone a day, how announcers worked on shifts in the train, if she felt any difficulty in broadcasting, and how many hours they broadcast a day. Asking her about these matters, he guessed what their trouble was.

Hearing that she used manuscripts and newspapers as the material for broadcasting, he estimated the size of a newspaper type with his finger tip and said: "**How hard it would be to read these small letters in a running train! It would be difficult to use newspapers for broadcasting.**"

Reading newspapers in the running train is, in fact, not an easy matter. However, train announcers, not to mention the officials in charge of train broadcast, got accustomed to it. Feeling sorry to have worried him, she said that sometimes she would use newspapers for broadcasting, but would generally receive manuscripts for reading practice one day before broadcasting.

Becoming more serious, however, he said to the officials:

"**Announcers spend a day to practise the reading of manuscripts for broadcasting. This cannot ensure the promptness of news. Promptness is vital to news report.**"

He continued: "**The train broadcast should ensure promptness, and this requires timely preparations of the manuscripts. Announcers should do reading practice as soon as they get the manuscripts, and report them promptly. If they use newspapers as texts for broadcasting they might possibly make blunders because the letters are too small, so they** should use the manuscripts for the purpose, except in special cases."

He then acquainted himself with the percentage of music and literary and art works in the entire train broadcasting programme, and looked carefully at the programme.

"**The train broadcast is very important,**" he said after thinking over the matter for a long while. "**The passengers are a huge mass of people.... Therefore, we can give extensive education to them through train broadcasting.**

"**At present no one is interested in this broadcasting, this is wrong,**" he went on. "**It must deal with lots of literary and art works. Only newspaper editorials and a bit of news would be advisable for the passengers, and much time should be devoted to literary and art works.**"

The statement was a guideline to illuminate the road the train broadcast must follow.

Listening to him, she could understand more keenly the importance of the train broadcast and made up her mind to do her job even better.

When she was absorbed in this thought, he pointed to a recording tape spool on the table, asking if there were only such small ones. She hurriedly took out a big one, regretting her failure to do so beforehand.

"**Well, you have big spools,**" he said, feeling relieved. "**Good. It needs a little longer time for literary and art works, so there must be such big recording tape spools.**"

Saying this, he read all the titles of songs written in small letters on the spool case.

He instructed the officials that the Radio and TV Broadcasting Committee should make copies of music well for the train broadcast, giving efficient guidance and assistance to it, and break all bottlenecks if it had any.

After a little while, he stood up and said to the officials:

"**The train broadcast must do a good job. Efforts must be devoted to this broadcast.**"

After gazing at the announcer with a tender look, he warmly shook her hand and encouraged her to work hard in good health. He left the studio, saying that he would have another opportunity to consider the work of the train broadcast separately.

As can be seen above, the dear leader visited the train broadcast studio with a deep understanding of its importance, and paid attention to all problems, however small, showing clearly the road to be followed by the train broadcast and looked after it constantly. Thanks to his sagacious leadership, our train broadcast is giving a free rein to its militant might as one of the powerful media for mass education.

Supporting New Buds

One day in early April 1974, the dear leader Comrade Kim Jong Il went over an article written by journalists of a publishing house about the revolutionary activities and achievements of President Kim Il Sung.

The article described impressive facts about all the burdens he had borne on his shoulders, visiting every nook and corner of the country to build a powerful land of bliss on earth, after he won national liberation as a result of many years of hard-fought battles. It also dealt skilfully with the scene in which he looked back with deep emotion on the days of anti-Japanese armed struggle as he sat in the car running along the Tuman River. This was a bright idea.

Giving high praise to this point, the dear leader then said:

"**In particular, the article described the President's course of local inspection tour and, finally, linked it with his** recollection of the days of anti-Japanese armed struggle in the car driving along the Tuman River. This is a bright idea.

"In this respect, the writers should be encouraged and highly estimated."

Taking scrupulous care of the journalists' writing, he would find out new buds among them, and support and assess them highly, thus developing their power of thinking and leading them to produce novel writings.

This encouragement and meticulous care stirred up creative enthusiasm in their hearts.

One July day of 1974, the Radio and TV Broadcasting Committee broadcasted a political essay, a new form of radio programme, with an aim of inspiring our working class and the rest of people to further innovations and creation.

Much pleased to listen to this political essay which was well adapted for radio, the dear leader said as follows:

"A radio political essay is one of the powerful weapons for ideological campaign. It integrates the essayist's writing and the eloquence of the announcer in informing the workers and officials clearly of the vital problem to be resolved at a given time. It shows them precisely where to stand and lets them know their weaknesses in time by carrying on an ideological campaign in accordance with the President's instructions and Party policy, so that all of them will be alert and active and resolute in the revolutionary struggle and construction work."

While encouraging the radio political essay, the dear leader gave meticulous guidance to develop it into one of the most powerful educational media to rouse the people to a more determined revolutionary struggle and the work of construction.

It was on a night several days before the national demonstration lecture on automation which he himself organized. At that time the journalists who were out at the Hwanghae Iron Works, one of the iron production bases, were writing a radio political essay for the participants in the lecture. However, they were irritated till late at night, for they started writing without selecting the definite seed.

Anticipating their problem, the dear leader instructed that the essay to be written must show the people a correct orientation and viewpoint on automation.

This was the very seed they failed to find out, though they were trying hard to do so all night to complete the political essay. They were greatly encouraged by the scrupulous care of the dear leader who regarded as a precious bud the radio political essay which the journalists themselves had considered merely a kind of ordinary article, and who even provided them with the seed to make it an effective means of disseminating Party policy.

The dear leader was also attentive to the reaction to the radio political essay on the part of those who participated in the demonstration lecture.

Reaffirming the effectiveness and influence of the radio political essay, the dear leader said:

"A worker who listened to the radio political essay is said to have commented that in former days whips were used to make people cry and work but today articles serve the purpose. This is precisely the strength of political work, the might of ideological campaign."

As you see, the dear leader highly appreciates even a small bright idea thought up by a journalist and gives a prominence to it so that it can bear good fruit in the implementation of Party policy. Thanks to his meticulous care and warm affection, our journalists are working with fervent creative enthusiasm, thinking up one new idea after another.

Seeing the Manuscripts for Announcers

On December 31, 1977, the dear leader Comrade Kim Jong Il took time off the tight schedule on the last day of the year to visit the Radio and TV Broadcasting Committee, on receiving the report that the project of a new radio hall was completed. He arrived there in the afternoon and cordially acknowledged the greetings of broadcasting workers, before stepping into the hall.

He looked carefully around every corner of the building with a feeling of a father calling at his son's new house. The hall still smelled of paint and lacquer and had many defects, due to the hasty completion of the project. However, he praised the initiative shown in the building of the hall, saying that it was fairly good.

He first dropped in at the editorial room for recording where he returned the greetings of the editors before inspecting newly-installed transcription machines and editing equipment one after another. Then he entered the recording studio where announcers were working. He complimented them on their work and shook hands warmly with two announcers, even before he was greeted.

He asked them what was recorded there and if they listened to their own voices while recording, and then told them to try. Having the infinite honour of speaking over the radio unexpectedly in his presence, they were joyful, when they took their seats in front of the microphone. He gave instructions for the door to be closed and motioned a cameraman beside him to put the lights on. He looked for a while at them recording their announcement in a dazzling light of illuminators. Then he picked up the manuscripts to turn over the pages one by one and asked them who wrote them, whether the announcers themselves or others.

They answered that they recorded the manuscripts prepared by journalists. Hearing this, he was concerned about the difficulty of reading others' handwritings. Indeed, this was the same affection as the fatherly leader had showed for the announcers when he visited the TV hall. The fatherly leader had seen their manuscripts, instructing that they should be written in large letters because now the letters were too small for them to read with ease.

Looking at the manuscripts again the dear leader expressed concern over the fact that newspaper editorials were printed in too small letters for the announcers to see when recording them, although the manuscripts dispatched by the Central News Agency were available for the purpose. Then he told an accompanying official earnestly that from now on there should be a system whereby the newspaper offices would make copies of editorials in a specially big type for the announcers and deliver them directly to the Radio and TV Broadcasting Committee. He also gave a valuable instruction on recording. He encouraged the announcers to work well, before he moved into another room.

Soon after his visit to the radio hall, the announcers became able to use copies in a specially large type when broadcasting editorials.

Thanks to the warm love and meticulous care of the dear leader who felt the announcers' embarrassment even when he saw them reading manuscripts in small type and ensured that copies printed specially in capitals be supplied, the announcers are proudly transmitting the voice of Chollima Korea to the whole world without any inconvenience.

Announcers' Attire

On November 10, 1978, the dear leader Comrade Kim Jong Il gave the officials concerned the orientation of information and propaganda to effect great upsurge in coal production, and pointed out the need to specify the time to telecast the programmes for miners.

According to this instruction, arrangements were made to broadcast such programmes twice a week so that vigorous productive efforts of colliers could be handled intensively.

On December 5, a TV soiree was held in the hour for colliers under the title, "The whole nation should vigorously assist the coal mines in the Anju district." At the soiree officials concerned expressed their resolutions to assist these mines, and colourful art performances were given.

The woman announcer who conducted this soiree was in colourful and gorgeous Korean costume. She introduced the vigorous labour efforts of the Anju miners and their brilliant successes, coupled with agitating remarks of calling upon all sectors to give effective assistance to them.

The dear leader who televiewed this scene realized at once that the announcer's dress did not match with the atmosphere of the soiree.

He rang up an official and told him:

"Why do telecasters in Korean attire appear in the programme for coal miners? They should wear Korean dresses in the news hour, but they had better put on simple dresses and act like agitators when encouraging people to increased production. The woman announcers appear in Korean attire every- where simply because they have been instructed to wear rich clothes. They should be dressed as required by the occasions—in Korean or other dresses."

Listening to him, the official clearly understood that announcers' attire did not fit the circumstances.

It was not until they received his teaching that announcers and leading workers in this sector were indeed sorry for not giving this item the study it warranted. Since then the announcers have paid close attention to dressing themselves to suit the programmes and circumstances.

The dear leader's brilliant insight penetrated everything from the announcers' dressing to diction—and corrected errors in time, thus leading them not to fall into any slightest deviation in their work.

Letting Cars Take a Roundabout Way to Provide Quiet Working Conditions for Journalists

On the evening of April 14, 1978, the dear leader Comrade Kim Jong Il took time to visit the *Rodong Sinmun* in spite of the pressure of work on the eve of the national holiday—the 66th birthday of the great leader Comrade Kim Il Sung.

Receiving greetings from the officials of the newspaper who came out to meet him, he kindly shook their hands one by one, and said that he had long planned to visit them but could not afford the time until now.

Making a round of the office, he gave valuable instructions and came out into the front yard. Dusk had already begun to fall. Standing there, he looked outside over the fence for a while.

He acquainted himself with what institutions were housed in the buildings on the other side of the road and listened to street noises. Then he asked what the situation was since he had taken steps to stop lorries passing by the newspaper office.

At the question, they could not conceal their astonishment. Originally, the road near that office building was busy. Lorries, trolleys, buses and cars ran in an unceasing stream and there were a throng of pedestrians. Therefore, it was impossible not to hear noises. But somehow there was no more lorry traffic there, street noises diminished considerably.

While writing articles in an unusually quiet atmosphere, the journalists of the Party paper did not know why lorry traffic was halted on the road in close proximity of their office. Only now they could understand the reason. It was the result of the efforts the dear leader had made on behalf of the journalists of the Party paper.

They suddenly remembered what happened one day in April of 1974. That day he summoned a leading official of the Party paper and said that the office building seemed to be unsuitable for the writers because of noises of vehicular traffic and a hotel situated nearby. Saying this he could not feel relieved. On a June day in the same year, he remarked that some day the hotel would be turned into sleeping quarters for the journalists working throughout the night. Unable to free himself from the anxiety, he saw to it that lorries took a roundabout way and that the hotel was turned as he suggested.

Still fixing his eyes over the highway as if listening to street noises, the dear leader continued:

"Lorries stopped to run along the road by the *Rodong Sinmun* and, from now on, buses should also be made to take another road. Then, silence will reign here, which will be a favourable working condition for the journalists."

Under his utmost care, trolley and other buses were made to take a roundabout way and the journalists became able to write and edit articles in a very quiet place.

Indeed, the dear leader is a benevolent teacher who regards as large even a trifling matter which journalists themselves cannot feel and shows profound solicitude to them.

GREAT LOVE

GREAT LOVE

GIVING PROMINENCE TO PRESSMEN

"Those Who Write in Accordance with the Party's Intention Are Heroes"

The dear leader Comrade Kim Jong Il said:

"Those who write in accordance with the Party's intention are heroes.

"I myself have written a great deal, and from my own experience I know that writing is most difficult. Therefore, those who treat, assign and write articles can be called heroes."

Literary pursuits have long appeared and there are innumerable writers in the world. However, they are not fighters who block the enemy's pillbox with their bodies. Throughout all generations, probably nobody had ever thought writers would be called heroes.

Nevertheless, here is a touching story which one cannot read without shedding a tear. It is a story about an old journalist who became a labour hero in his sixties.

It was April 13, 1982 when the whole country was in a festive mood greeting the 70th birthday of the respected leader Comrade Kim Il Sung as the most auspicious event of the nation.

That day the editorial staff of the *Rodong Sinmun* were busy at their work in excitement, seeking for a better way to write eulogies of the entire Korean people to the respected

Comrade Kim Il Sung, the great revolutionary leader and benevolent father, who has performed immortal exploits in the history of our nation and mankind.

At the very moment, they unexpectedly received the happy, stirring news that the dear leader got the titles of honour and state orders awarded to journalists and editors of the Party newspaper on the occasion of the great leader's 70th birthday. The news spread throughout the newspaper office, turning it instantaneously into a turmoil of great delight and deep emotion. This delight and emotion was added by the sensational news that the title of Labour Hero was awarded to a pressman who was carrying on editing work even in his late sixties.

The moment the decree of the Central People's Committee on awarding the title of Labour Hero to him was announced, he covered his face with his hands, filled with surging excitement.

Indeed, it was a happy moment that only those living under a great leader could experience.

This auspicious event was the first of its kind in nearly 40 years of the Party newspaper, nay, in the history of the press of our country.

Thanks to the boundlessly warm love of the dear leader who calls writers heroes and gives them the greatest prominence, a legend-like story of an ordinary pressman becoming a writer hero has appeared in the world. Such a happy event could not be found elsewhere.

He became a labour hero, the highest honour of the citizen, neither at a production centre nor construction site where feats of labour were performed through great creation and innovations. It was simply a press organ. He was just an old journalist who had devoted his all silently to the Party newspaper. He had only striven to write articles for the Party newspaper and edit it as the great leader and the dear leader wished.

However, the dear leader recommended him as hero, though he was over sixty, and had his breast adorned with a gold medal, believing that he would devote the remainder of his life to the Party newspaper as before.

Thanks to the trust and love of the dear leader who regards writers as heroes, he had been bestowed with the high honour of the "Kim Il Sung Prize" and now became the first hero in the press of our country.

None of the journalists of the Party newspaper was outside the reach of the dear leader's warm love. A deputy editor-in-chief was awarded the "Kim Il Sung Prize", some pressmen became People's Journalists or Merited Journalists and others received high state orders.

"Kim Il Sung Prize", Labour Hero, People's Journalist and Merited Journalist—how high and honourable these titles are!

The dear leader who has attached great importance to the Party paper, values the successes of the reporters and editors who have served the paper in good faith and gratified and satisfied the great leader and the Party through their writing and editing activities, and regards their achievements as a distinguished service in strengthening our Party and advancing our revolution. Therefore, these honourable titles are a crystallization of the infinitely deep solicitude and great paternal love of the dear leader.

Highly Praising Even a Small Success

One day in July 1974, an official came to the dear leader's office, taking a copy of the paper *Pyongyang Sinmun* with him, to report on the work of his newspaper.

The dear leader put aside what he had been doing and

unfolded the newspaper. Giving a close look at the paper, he stopped at an article carried on the second and third pages and carefully scrutinized it. It was entitled *Let Us Transform Ourselves after the Immortal Juche Idea of the Great Leader*.

This was a special article dealing with experiences. Reporters and editors of this newspaper, pursuant to the policy of modelling the whole of society on the Juche idea, advanced by the dear leader, had gone to a factory and helped workers and technicians set an example in carrying out this policy, working together with them and, on this basis, wrote about their experiences.

Informed of this from the official, the dear leader was very satisfied and highly praised the pressmen of the *Pyongyang Sinmun* for the help they had given to the factory, a very laudable deed.

He resumed and was minutely studying the fourth page. This page carried various items—the news of artists of the Korean February 8th Film Studio on outdoor shooting, news on sports and science, introduction of a pleasure ground in the making, hygienic knowledge, guide to the theatres, radio and television programmes and so on.

With a bright smile, the dear leader skimmed over the fourth page for a while and then expressed great satisfaction, saying that he could see the pressmen were striving to improve the editing of the newspaper as the Party wanted.

He continued to say:

"You tell the pressmen of the *Pyongyang Sinmun* that the Party centre has read today's issue of the paper and highly commended them for their laudable deed."

When the dear leader's compliment was conveyed to them, the reporters and editors of the *Pyongyang Sinmun* recalled what had happened some time before.

It was November 2, 1973.

The dear leader was pleased more than anyone else with

the fact that journalists of the *Pyongyang Sinmun* made a substantial contribution to bringing about a great upsurge in the production of consumer goods. Upholding the great leader's instructions to increase production of sundry goods, they had helped to initiate "the struggle of loyalty for general goods production" as a mass movement, and popularized it throughout the country. At that time, too, the dear leader said in praise of them: **"Well done. You *Pyongyang Sinmun* journalists have performed a meritorious deed."**

The dear leader's repeated high praise of every small success achieved by the pressmen is expressive of his ardent desire to encourage them by giving them social prominence.

Therefore, whenever the dear leader shows them great love, our pressmen are greatly encouraged by it and make a firm resolution to live up to his great political trust and deep concern by writing more and better articles.

On New Year's Day

It was the New Year's Day of 1974.

The snow was falling in larger flakes than ever before, as if greeting the New Year.

That day the chief official of the Party paper *Rodong Sinmun* was busy compiling the paper from early morning, when he was unexpectedly called up by the dear leader.

When he came, the dear leader cordially welcomed him with New Year greetings and kindly asked if the newspapermen were enjoying the New Year's Day cheerfully and what they were doing that day.

On the previous night, journalists of the Party newspaper had received precious gifts from the dear leader.

They hurried to the office on the early morning and set about their work. They were devoting themselves to fully show on the first issue of the new year the strong spirit of our people who turned out in the struggle to carry out the highly important task put forth by the great leader in his New Year address. That day everyone in the newspaper office was enthusiastically working. Some of them went on official business carrying suitcases and cameras, and others were giving full play to their collective knowledge to edit the newspaper better.

Informed of such situation from the official, the dear leader stood up from his chair, drew near the officials present there and said in a rumbling voice:

"Look. We are all enjoying a holiday like this, but the staff of the Party paper are even working today. They are taking such trouble."

His words expressed the loving feeling of real parents who are eager to give prominence to their commendable son.

After a short pleasant chat with the officials, the dear leader rose from his seat proposing to have a photograph taken in memory of the New Year's Day. All posed for a photograph, with high honour and great joy. The chief official of the Party paper also took his place in a hurry.

The dear leader who was approaching his seat, came to a sudden stop looking for someone among the officials. When he found the official from the Party paper, the dear leader called him to come near him.

Without seeing the reason he obeyed the dear leader, and was at a loss what to do. The dear leader drew him by the arm to his side.

The official could not find words how to thank the dear leader who sent gifts to the staff members of the Party paper on every holiday and offered them such an honourable place as this. When all the officials sat around a table after the photos were taken, the dear leader proposed a toast to success in the work of all the staff members of *Rodong Sinmun* and to their health.

Indeed, his toast was a crystallization of love and trust with which he gives so much prominence to the journalists of the Party newspaper.

Deep Concern for Establishment of the Broadcast Day

One day in the latter part of August 1970, the dear leader Comrade Kim Jong Il was quite busy giving guidance to enormous work related with the preparations for the Fifth Party Congress. Nevertheless, he considered that the 25th anniversary of the inauguration of the broadcast (October 14) was drawing near and called a leadership official of the Radio and TV Broadcasting Committee to visit him.

When the official entered his office with deep emotion and excitement, the dear leader who was reading a pile of documents, warmly welcomed him and asked about his health and work. Then he told him:

"Since the Radio and TV Broadcasting Committee will greet the 25th anniversary of the inauguration of its broadcast this year, you had better hold a memorial ceremony. The inauguration was indeed an event of great significance.

"That our broadcasting proclaimed its birth by diffusing to the whole world the General's speech on his triumphant return is a great event in its history and the highest honour for our broadcasting workers....

"We should make good preparations for the 25th anniversary so as to make it a great festival of broadcasting workers."

Keeping deep in his mind every word of the dear leader's instructions, the official was stirred to strong emotions.

The broadcasting anniversary was nothing but a small annual ceremony of a single establishment, compared with the Fifth Party Congress which would be a great event in the history of our Party's struggle.

Nevertheless, the dear leader explained in detail how to conduct the ceremony and on what scale so as to celebrate the broadcasting anniversary magnificently, though he was very busy preparing for the Party Congress.

His words were expressive of his deep trust and warm love for broadcasting workers.

Full of gratitude for the dear leader's great solicitude, the broadcasting workers were hurrying with their preparations for celebrating the 25th anniversary in a grand style.

One day, the dear leader again called up an official of the Radio and TV Broadcasting Committee and asked about the preparations. Feeling his deep concern for the celebration, the official hesitated for a little while before he replied that they had formed a preparatory group for the ceremony and were drawing up the report and other documents. Having heard his answer carefully, the dear leader said:

"You should make good preparations for the celebration of the 25th anniversary of national radio.

"In my opinion, it is advisable to institute the Broadcast Day on this occasion."

Establishment of the Broadcast Day would be an auspicious event that would go down throughout the history of broadcasting. Thanks to the great leader's solicitude, the state had instituted many significant festival days—the Miners' Day, the Fishermen's Day, the Education Day and so on, not to speak of national holidays.

But nobody had ever thought of establishing the Broadcast Day for broadcasting workers who number not many even throughout the whole country.

This could be done only by the dear leader who had attached great importance to the place and role of broadcasting in the revolutionary struggle and construction work and provided everything for its development.

When the official thanked him in an emotional tone, the dear leader continued to say:

"**National radio started diffusion on the historic day when the great leader made a speech on his triumphant return, so it is advisable to set this day as the Broadcast Day and commemorate it as a traditional holiday every year.**"

His concern was not limited to this. Knowing the ardent desire of broadcasting workers, the dear leader honoured them highly by inviting the great leader to their ceremony, and accorded them privileges by choosing the Pyongyang Grand Theatre with thousands of seats as the meeting place instead of the originally planned Moranbong Theatre.

Some time later, the dear leader examined personally the documents relating to the celebration and gave instructions to commend officially meritorious broadcasting workers and invite local broadcasting workers to the ceremony.

As we have seen, the dear leader took into consideration every small and big problem related to the celebration—its size and venue, the contents of documents, commendation, the participants, etc.—and gave important instructions and showed deep concern.

Thanks to the great efforts of the dear leader, the celebration of the 25th anniversary of the inauguration of the broadcast was grandly held as an event of historical significance.

In the presence of the respected leader Comrade Kim Il Sung the broadcasting workers posed for a photograph, held the celebration and saw the performance. All the while they expressed unbounded thanks to the dear leader who had provided them with this opportunity.

Following the establishment of the Broadcast Day, the

dear leader instituted the Press Day, the first of its kind in this field.

Indeed, the dear leader Comrade Kim Jong Il is a benefactor and a great teacher who places the pressmen at the zenith of happiness and glory.

TO TRAIN JOURNALISTS FAITHFUL TO THE PARTY

A Copy of the Great Leader's Work Presented to an Official

In February 1968, an official of the Radio and TV Broadcasting Committee had the honour of being summoned by the dear leader Comrade Kim Jong Il to work for several days, by his side.

One day the dear leader presented the official with a copy of the great leader's work *On the 20th Anniversary of the Founding of the Korean People's Army* which he himself had just received. Moved by the kindness the dear leader had shown in presenting such a valuable document, the official could hardly repress his emotions. At the same time the dear leader pointed out:

"A diligent study of the great leader's works will enable you to have an accurate understanding of the policy he has outlined.

"You must be well acquainted with the situation. Otherwise, you may be ignorant of the reality.

"The situation is very tense now. This tense and complex situation demands that you work more with a thorough understanding of the great leader's revolutionary ideas and Party policy. In this condition you must study harder. One who has studied a good deal will not vacillate ideologically. But one who neglects his studies, while loitering about, is weak in ideological will."

This remark contained the dear leader's high intention and warm affection to induce the official to live for ever as a revolutionary fighter of the great leader and add luster to his political integrity which was given by the leader. Bearing these words deep in his mind, the official was so overwhelmed with excitement that he was unable to thank the dear leader.

He made a firm resolution to work for the realization of the thoughts and intentions of the great leader and the dear leader, to the best of his ability and with lasting loyalty.

Afterwards, on meeting the official who was going on a tour abroad, the dear leader again showed him his warm affection.

The dear leader Comrade Kim Jong Il said:

"You must never fail to repay the Party for its trust and care. Without the warm care of the great leader, nothing is significant. You should not think that because you are handsome, you are free to do as you like.

"We must find a life worth living in our vigorous efforts to lighten the burden from the mind of the great leader."

If he had lived under Japanese imperialist rule, the official, who was an orphan, would have been forsaken by humanity. However, the dear leader had brought him up, not only to be a member of the glorious Workers' Party of Korea and a capable cameraman, but was also striving to train him into a most honourable and true revolutionary of our time. Enjoying such a great affection and trust from the dear leader, the official felt immensely proud.

The official is going on stoutly on the road of loyalty amid the infinite love and trust of the dear leader.

Journalists Must Read Books More Than Anyone Else

One day in October 1962, the artists in Pyongyang gave a music and dance performance in the presence of the great leader Comrade Kim Il Sung at the Pyongyang Grand Theatre.

A journalist of the Central News Agency went to the theatre to cover the news. While seeing the performance, he kept trying to conceive the idea and form of his article, and as soon as an act came to an end, he opened his scribbling book.

At that moment a functionary hurried to him and informed him that he was summoned by the dear leader. He went with a throbbing heart to the lounge where the dear leader was.

On seeing him, the dear leader, with a bright smile, warmly shook the hand of the journalist who was bowing politely. Then he asked the journalist if he had finished his news coverage and if he had any problems.

The journalist could not hide his emotions at this warm affection shown to him, after all he was only a mediocre pressman whom the dear leader had met for a short time several months before when he was performing his duty.

The dear leader asked him about the points of the article, which he was reporting. He replied that he was going to write about the programme and the content of the performance.

The dear leader then told him that he should not confine himself to the introduction of the programme but must emphasize the fact that our art was flowering and developing as we witnessed today, in keeping with the great leader's Juche-based idea on literature and art.

On hearing the dear leader's words, the journalist blushed, for he realized that he might have possibly missed a crux in his article because he had covered the news not from a political viewpoint but from the standpoint of a simple conveyor of news.

In order to make him feel at ease, the dear leader told him to sit down and then kindly asked him how many hours he spent a day to study.

The newsman, with his head bowed, could not answer offhand. Then the dear leader said with a light smile on his face: "**Journalists must read books more than anyone else and make study their regular habit.**" His voice was low and gentle, but the journalist listened to it with great emotion.

Though he often talked about the importance of study, the newsman shunned study with the excuse that he had no time to study due to the pressure of work. He felt remorseful at the thought of the dear leader kindly advising him to study hard, instead of blaming him.

The dear leader stated that in their studies the journalists must attach great importance to the great leader's revolutionary thoughts, and pointed out:

"**In particular, you must profoundly study the leader's works and thus acquaint yourselves thoroughly with their content. Only then you will be able to successfully carry out information activities in accordance with the leader's thoughts and intentions.**"

Not forgetting the dear leader's statement, the newsman keenly realized that making a study of the great leader's works was vital to him, after all, if he was to uphold his honour by working faithfully for the leader.

The dear leader went on saying that by studying the Party's policies earnestly he would be able to judge all questions from a political point of view and write fine articles, answer in complicated realities the questions to be solved by the Party in a given period and arouse the masses for their realization.

A bell rang announcing the start of part two of the performance. The dear leader shook the pressman's hand warmly and said, in an affectionate voice, that he must become an excellent journalist through intensive study.

The newsman bowed to the dear leader with feelings of high respect for him. He repented of his mistaken idea that he was unable to write good articles due to the lack of "good material", and he firmly resolved to become an excellent journalist through studying as instructed by the dear leader.

He was not the only newsman who took the new step into this direction after receiving valuable teachings from the dear leader.

On May 2, 1965, a distinguished African guest on a visit to our country gave a banquet in honour of the great leader at the Okryu Restaurant.

At the banquet hall the dear leader summoned a woman journalist of the news agency who was there to take a news coverage. He offered her a seat, saying that she must have had much trouble to report the function. And then he asked the name of the university she had graduated from. Hearing that she was then learning through a correspondence course of Kim Il Sung University, the dear leader said that she must have trouble in studying while working, and asked about the subjects she was studying.

She mentioned the great leader's revolutionary history and works, Party policy, literature, etc. The dear leader told her that a profound study of the great leader's revolutionary history would enable her to reflect extensively the glorious root of our Party in her articles.

The dear leader added that she must draw on the revolutionary habit of anti-Japanese guerrillas for study and creation, to write more articles for the education of the working people. Meanwhile, he inspired her with confidence, saying that she would be able to write as many good articles as she wanted, if she steadily mastered the writing method while reading novels as well as the editorials and political essays of the Party newspaper.

The dear leader lost some of his precious time in teaching her in detail the ways to study, with the purpose of training a young reporter to be a fine journalist. Moved by his great kindness, she could hardly calm down and resolved to come up to his great expectations and return his benevolent affection without fail.

Until They Have Grown Up into Editorial Writers

On April 14, 1978, the dear leader gave on-the-spot guidance to the *Rodong Sinmun*, where he expressed great satisfaction at the fact that the Party paper established its authority, and he pointed out:

"**Writings in the Party paper have also been put on the right track. In the past they were long with a poor content, but now they are short and contain rich material. Editorials and other leading articles in particular are excellent.**"

The officials and journalists of the newspaper were greatly moved by the great affection of the dear leader who had accorded all the honours to the editorial writers, disregarding his efforts in teaching and leading the journalists. These writers had traversed a worthwhile revolutionary road under the dear leader's warm care.

On December 26, 1973, the dear leader said:

"**It is advisable that the newspapers carry articles in which they unfailingly hold the President in high esteem, adore him** and praise him as the great revolutionary leader."

This remark served as a very important guideline that clarified the stand the journalists should adopt in their writing.

The journalists made a firm resolution to write editorials and other leading articles in conformity with the Party's intentions by following the example of the dear leader's infinite loyalty to the great leader.

In February 1974, the dear leader personally organized the work of bringing about a revolutionary change in the writing of editorials and trained and led the editorial writers in their worthwhile work.

On February 12, 1974—the day before the historic Eighth Plenary Meeting of the Fifth Party Central Committee was over—the dear leader gave the Party paper an honourable task of writing an editorial on the plenary meeting within that day and editing it, along with the report of the closing session.

With great emotions the journalists quickly wrote the editorial and completed it in half a day.

The dear leader personally examined the first proof of the editorial *Let the Whole Party, the Whole Country and the Entire People be Mobilized in the Great Work of Socialist Construction in Response to the Call of the Great Leader and the Appeal of the Party Centre!* and told the editorial staff to carry an editorial in the paper every day from a different angle. His words infinitely stirred up the officials and editorial staff of the Party paper.

It was too much for them to write every day a long editorial on the policy with such a limited staff. However, they got down to the task with a wholehearted desire to come up to the great expectations of the dear leader and justify his confidence. After making elaborate arrangements, they completed an editorial in a day, and sometimes even in half a day, which before had taken them ten or fifteen days. In this course, they acquired the revolutionary traits of sensitively accepting the Party's policies and explaining and propagating them in a lightning manner.

The dear leader found precious time to examine their editorials and correct their shortcomings, leading them to produce excellent editorials.

He made no less than 16 alterations in the first proof of the editorial dated May 25, 1974, *Let Us Imbue the Whole Society with the Great Juche Idea.*

The dear leader omitted the term "ideological campaign" from the editorial in which the newsmen had used "speed campaign" and "ideological campaign" in a line without distinguishing between them. Then he pointed out that since the ideological campaign, lightning operation and finish-one-by-one tactics were embodiments of the speed campaign, they must not be used as co-ordinate concepts. In addition, he replaced the words "wicked virus" with "miscellaneous spirits" as expressed by the great leader for reactionary ideas such as capitalism, revisionism and flunkeyism. Lest his corrections made in the marginal space of the proof sheet should be unintelligible to the newsmen, the dear leader lost no time to explain them one by one.

Sometimes he put novel expressions such as the "drumbeat of revolution" in the drafting proofs so that the newsmen of the Party paper might always write fresh editorials.

In this way, the dear leader showed a meticulous concern for them to write good editorials, and whenever they wrote excellent ones, he highly appreciated them. However, when they failed to make good progress in the writing of editorials, resting on their laurels, he sternly rebuked them.

On December 13, 1979 when he saw a poor editorial of the Party paper, the dear leader said sternly that the quality of editorial was lower than before, probably because he was not as strong in his demand for the writing as previously, limiting his efforts to the correction of expressions due to the pressure of work.

Informed of his words, the pressmen seriously reviewed their work and made strenuous efforts, with the result that they produced in succession good editorials commensurate with the demand of the Party policy.

Stressing that the pressmen must study hard to write fine editorials in accordance with the Party's intentions, the dear leader showed concern for them to study enough.

One day in February 1977, the dear leader called in one of the officials concerned and said that the writers of editorials and other leading articles should be encouraged to study to imbue themselves with the Party policy even if they would produce their works less often.

Boundlessly inspired by the dear leader's particular concern for them, they energetically studied the great leader's works and Party documents under a minute plan, thus elevating their political and practical qualifications.

Under this tender guidance, full of love, the pressmen of the Party paper have grown up in a period of only a few years, to be competent journalists capable of readily writing long and important editorials in line with the Party's intentions.

"Make Yourself a Prominent Woman Journalist"

One evening in late July 1964, a woman journalist of the *Pyongyang Sinmun* was coming home with a light heart from the office. As she left the main street and was walking homeward, a car passing by stopped suddenly. She was surprised at the sight of the car, as the dear leader unexpectedly got down from it. He beckoned her to come and advanced to her and shook her warmly by the hand. He kindly asked her if she was going home and whether the work was beyond her limits. She simply answered in the negative.

Laughing broadly, he said: **"When people do with a determination what they want to do, they do not feel any sign of tiredness."** Then he learned in detail how she was working. She told him that due to her poor practical qualifications as a new journalist who had graduated from a university several months before, she could not produce any good writings worth mentioning. Hearing her, he said: **"You must not think that new journalists cannot write good articles. Experience is of course necessary, but the question is that you must observe the reality from the point of view of the leader's teachings and the Party policy and find out the point at issue from it. Journalists should keenly observe and judge any phenomenon from the political point of view. Only then they can make a clear statement."**

Saying this, the dear leader kindly encouraged her to get down to work with daring and write a quantity of good articles which would help arouse Party members and working people to implement Party policies, instead of falling into timidity and passivism in the writing of articles because of her brief journalistic life.

At the moment she could picture in her mind the events of the past when he was so anxious and meticulously concerned to bring her up to be a writer.

It was several years before that the dear leader came to make the acquaintance of her. At that time he found in a young girl a new bud of talent for writing. From then on, in order to bring this small bud into bloom, he taught her the method of writing and examined her raw writing till after midnight to complete it. In this way he cultivated her talent and took care of her. When she was assigned to the *Pyongyang Sinmun* after graduating from the university, he rejoiced over it and inspired her by saying that he hoped to see her name frequently in that newspaper.

Always remembering these matters, the dear leader saw her on the way home and stopped, though very busy, to show concern for her. Wrapped up in boundless happiness, she stood motionless for a long time, looking at the disappearing car.

His affection and trust stirred up her enthusiasm.

She wrote articles with full confidence, exploiting news sources at a factory one day and in the countryside the next.

One day in the late spring of 1965, the dear leader summoned her again to acquaint himself with her writing activities, though he was busy with his work. He asked her in detail if she felt any difficulty in writing and what articles she had written until that day. Then he told her that journalists must be better informed of reality than anybody else and that they must learn to judge and appraise it rightly. He added that they should study hard to know well the reality and write important articles, before pointing out:

"Journalists should arm themselves more thoroughly with the great leader's revolutionary ideas than anybody else. They must have a thorough knowledge of all his teachings, and regard them as the yardstick in covering data or writing articles."

Inspired by his affectionate instructions, she expressed her resolve to study deeply and grasp the great leader's revolutionary ideas and become a competent journalist having a high degree of knowledge.

After listening to her resolution in delight, he told her: **"Try as you make up your mind."**

From that time on, he read all her articles carried in the *Pyongyang Sinmun* without omission.

Early in December 1966 the dear leader summoned her in his office and told her that whenever he saw her name in the newspaper, he was glad, and that some time before he read her account about a meeting between a children's partisan leader and pupils in the city.

At that time she had considered articles must be long. So she told him that she felt ashamed of her articles because they were all short and insignificant.

Hearing her out, the dear leader remarked that writers were now trying only to produce great compositions. He continued:

"**You must produce great works not in terms of the length of articles but in their profound content.**

"**In our life, too, there are cases in which we cannot do a great work for lack of a small thing.**

"**As I said before, even a short article will be able to settle a great issue if it raises a new problem and gives a correct answer.**"

He also told her that she could never arouse the people by re-echoing hearsay and that she must write good articles by raising her qualifications.

His troubles, for a female journalist, knew no bounds.

One day in December 1966, he heard about her marriage. He summoned her again with anxiety about her future writing activity, as a housewife.

That day he got a detailed account of her home life and listened to her simple determination.

"**You must make yourself a prominent woman journalist as you have already resolved.**" He encouraged her in a trustful tone. "**I will give you an active help.**"

Indeed, the great pains taken by the dear leader for the making of an ordinary woman journalist are associated with his lofty desire and kindness to bring up the journalists to be not only politically sound, but also competent by raising their skill level.

Affection for an Announcer

In February 1978, there was an announcer who could not fall asleep throughout the night. He was taken into a sickroom of a leading hospital in the capital city of Pyongyang. He was an announcer in charge of overseas broadcast of the Radio and TV Broadcasting Committee. He was just transferred here under the care of the dear leader, after receiving treatment in a local hospital.

The more he remembered about it, the more he felt as if in a dream. As he thought of the affection of the dear leader, which increased with the lapse of time, the unforgettable days when he had grown up under the utmost care of the dear leader floated like a picture.

Although he had enjoyed the affection of the dear leader for many years, he could and would never forget the affection of New Year's Day more than ten years before.

That day he happened to spend the holiday alone. He could not but feel lonely due to longing for his mother. But he was given a great favour which he could not imagine even in a dream.

On the evening of December 31, an official called on him without notice. The official seized him by the shoulder and told him that the dear leader had wanted him to come quickly to celebrate the New Year's Day with him in his residence.

The announcer went in a hurry to the residence of the dear leader. When he was about to enter the garden, he came to a full halt. In the garden the dear leader stood waiting for him, in the falling snow.

Seeing this, he could not extend his New Year greetings to the dear leader. He only bowed before him.

The dear leader welcomed him with joy, shaking his hand warmly.

And then he said that it was a wonderful night, the snow falling in large flakes as if congratulating them. Then he led the announcer into the room.

Time passed amidst infinite joy and happiness of his greeting the New Year together with the dear leader. A watch-night bell rang announcing the commencement of the new year 1962.

The dear leader said with a broad smile:

"In the new year you must work and study harder to become a revolutionary soldier loyal to the great leader," as he offered a toast to the announcer.

The announcer could not suppress his emotion at the warm affection of the dear leader, who had guided the announcer step by step in the past so that he could begin a political life and work for overseas broadcast and who personally gave him his greetings for a Happy New Year with such a warm fatherly love.

When the announcer felt embarrassed and told him that he would now go home, the dear leader told him kindly that it was New Year's Day, at the same time asking him why he was so impatient.

While working amid such a great trust and affection, the announcer committed a grievous error in April that year. He could tell nobody about his mental agony.

One day the dear leader called in the announcer and treated him warmly as before. He then put his hand on the announcer's shoulder telling him, **"Mental agony would take you nowhere. So, let's sit and discuss the matter."**

The announcer felt sorry about committing a serious error, instead of repaying the dear leader for his great favour, and told the dear leader of his determination to toughen himself by physical labour.

The dear leader was silent for a while, lost in deep thought, before he spoke highly of the announcer's resolution and expressed his support to it. The dear leader inspired him by stating that he must be deliberate in any problem and, once he made up his mind, behave with determination. He said encouragingly that training through labour was not bad.

Deeply moved by the benevolent love of the dear leader who had put aside a great deal of important work to show him the way to make a fresh start, the announcer burst into tears.

The dear leader summoned again the announcer the day before he left for his destination. While having a meal together, he expressed great confidence and expectation, saying that he must work hard on the new post in good health and write to him as soon as he settled down.

Under such a meticulous care the announcer had trained himself and came back again to the post of broadcaster.

The announcer was deeply moved as he was looking back on all the affections of the past.

From the following day he was given intensive medical treatment by competent doctors and professors.

The dear leader was often informed about the progress of the announcer's medical treatment through a relevant official and personally sent tonics efficacious for the cure of his disease.

The announcer who had recovered his health after a treatment of a month's duration and stood again before a microphone, worked hard to repay the great solicitude shown to him by the dear leader.

On October 10, 1980, the announcer had the honour of delivering a foreign language broadcast at the historic Sixth Congress of the Workers' Party of Korea.

When the great leader Comrade Kim Il Sung and the dear leader Comrade Kim Jong Il took the platform of the congress, the announcer shouted cheers time and again, forgetting that he was standing before the microphone.

No sooner had the great leader and the dear leader been elected to the executives of the congress amid thunderous cheers, than the announcer, with a loyal heart, respectfully broadcast their honourable names to foreigners.

At dawn on October 15 when the announcer returned home after successfully fulfilling his duty for the congress, an official called at his house.

Some time later, a car carrying the announcer arrived at the place where the dear leader was.

Receiving the announcer with a radiant smile, the dear leader said that he was sorry to have called him in at dawn, and went on: "As I had been told that you would cover the First Plenary Meeting of the Sixth Party Central Committee in a foreign language broadcast yesterday, I listened to it through a receiver. You carried it out excellently."

He added: "Yesterday the head of a foreign delegation came to see me and asked where we had found such an excellent interpreter and whether we had invited him from a foreign country. I replied, He is a Korean and there is no need for us to invite interpreters from foreign countries. We settle everything ourselves if our revolution demands it. He is a Korean who was given Juche-based education at Kim Il Sung University. Don't you know the Juche-oriented educational theses? On hearing me, the head was deeply moved with admiration."

The announcer was at a loss what to do with the repeated praise of the dear leader. He was greatly excited.

The dear leader had shared joys and sorrows with him and steadily led him along a road of worthwhile struggle.

He could not find words to express the feeling of thanks for the great affection shown to him.

Nevertheless, the dear leader took his hand warmly, saying with great joy that the announcer had been really wonderful in broadcasting.

Concern for Training the Reserve of Journalists

On April 14, 1978, the day before the 66th birthday of the great leader Comrade Kim Il Sung, the most auspicious national holiday, the dear leader Comrade Kim Jong Il gave on-the-spot guidance to the *Rodong Sinmun*. With deep concern he went through the question of training the reserve of journalists.

The dear leader said:

"**You should train a large reserve of journalists. I have stressed it on several occasions, but you still pay little attention to it.**

"**Unless you bring up a reserve of journalists in a planned way, you will not be able to constantly replenish the ranks of journalists and steadily improve the quality of the newspaper.**"

Then, he asked the functionaries if they had recruited many young people.

One of them told him that the Party newspaper had received scores of university graduates. The dear leader remarked that the recruits would be able to write good articles, only after making an effort for a certain period of time.

The dear leader asked the vice-editors how many of these university graduates were able to write fine articles on their assignment. Then he repeatedly emphasized the need of training a large number of pressmen.

The officials were deeply impressed by the extraordinary intelligence, deep insight and noble affection of the dear leader who was meticulous not only in his guidance of the editorial work in hand but also in handling the question of intensifying the training of the reserve for continued improvement of the newspaper.

He asked the vice-editors' opinion on letting themselves and other journalists deliver special lectures at Kim Il Sung University.

He added that now the *Rodong Sinmun* was little concerned about the education of students at Kim Il Sung University but, in their graduation season, it would hasten to receive the good ones.

The officials felt the remorse for their neglect of training the reserve of journalists while keeping themselves busy by editing the newspaper.

Having fully understood the feelings of the repenting officials, however, the dear leader did not press his point. He said that as the newspaper had several vice-editors and many pressmen who were good at writing, their special lectures at the university, if realized, would be appreciated by teachers and students alike because they could be taught plenty of new things. He exhorted the vice-editors to deliver, in turn, a special lecture at the journalism course, the Korean Language Faculty, Kim Il Sung University, once every quarter. He also encouraged other journalists to do the same.

While listening to the dear leader saying about training the reserve of journalists, the officials and pressmen of this newspaper felt how great his confidence in them was. They firmly resolved to come up to his expectations and justify his confidence without fail.

They are now giving special lectures to the students of the journalism course of Kim Il Sung University regularly, as instructed by the dear leader, so that all of them may become competent journalists well versed in the press and with a high degree of political views and writing ability.

The dear leader has seen to it that the students of this course conduct practical work in many press establishments to improve their writing ability. He has also given these students the privilege to take the books concerning the theory on the press and other various publications.

Under the wise guidance and warm care of the dear leader, a reliable reserve of journalists are steadily being brought up to work for our publications.

FOR BETTER WORKING CONDITIONS

Offering a Choice

One early spring morning in 1968, an official of the photo department of the *Rodong Sinmun* was summoned by the dear leader Comrade Kim Jong Il to his office at the Party Central Committee.

"I would like to make you a good present today," said the dear leader receiving him cordially with a bright smile, as he led the official to his desk.

The cameraman looked at the desk, where he saw the latest and best cameras which he had never seen or seldom heard of.

"Choose whichever you like," the dear leader said in a tender voice, but the official hesitated.

After a while he took a camera and held it carefully in his hands.

Beaming affectionately the dear leader looked at the man, who was in a fit of excitement, and then said:

"We made many inquiries about good cameras for the *Rodong Sinmun*, but we were unable to find any. These we have obtained today."

These words reminded him of the dear leader who had been looking anxiously at the man's camera when they had been to Songnim several months before.

On November 11, 1967, the great leader was making a

historic speech at the meeting of the electors of the Songnim constituency.

The cameraman was intent on carrying out the honourable task of covering the great leader's revolutionary activity.

The respected President began his historic speech, and the cameraman took the picture and was coming down from the platform. He was beckoned by the dear leader Comrade Kim Jong Il who was sitting in the front row of the audience. As he greeted him politely, the dear leader motioned to the seat next to his. The man humbly took a seat a little away from him. But the dear leader gently told him to take the seat next to him and said in a low voice: **"Now, have a rest before you go on shooting."**

Choked with emotion, the cameraman just kept fingering his camera, unable to say anything.

The dear leader carefully looked at the man's camera. After a while he asked in a worried tone: **"Why? Is that the best one available for the Party paper?"**

Not knowing what he really meant, the man replied that it was a very good camera. In fact, the man was thinking that the camera was one of the best, so he could not understand why the dear leader was so anxious about the camera, which he was using to take the precious picture of the great leader.

The dear leader was concerned so much over the fact that the great leader's noble image was not photographed with the best camera the modern science and technology could offer.

Since then the dear leader had personally studied the best cameras in the world and ensured that the best of them were obtained. As soon as these cameras were brought to him, the dear leader called in the man.

Grasping the man's hand, the dear leader said as follows: **"You must take many good photographs with this camera.**

"In particular, you must reproduce truthful and vivid pictures related with the revolutionary activities of the great

leader by taking them in the required dimensions and carry them in the Party paper with respect so that his image will remain for ever in the minds of all people.

"I believe you will carry in the Party paper the precious images of the great leader better and more respectfully."

In reply to his earnest words the man pledged himself to loyalty from the bottom of his heart.

Innovations started in the work of the photo department of the Party paper which had received the gift from the dear leader.

The noble images of the great leader carried in the Party paper became tangibly larger in their dimensions and looked more respectful.

A week after he sent the camera, the dear leader personally rang up the *Rodong Sinmun* and asked in detail if they used the camera, whether they liked it, and if it produced good photographs.

At the report that the camera produced good photographs he was very satisfied and encouraged them to produce many more good pictures.

Concern over a Cameraman's Legwork

One day in late December 1974, the dear leader Comrade Kim Jong Il entrusted a cameraman of the Central News Agency with an assignment to accompany the great leader who was going on a local trip with a head of state from far-off Africa.

When the man was hurrying excitedly with his preparations for the trip, another exciting news was conveyed to him by an official.

A few hours before, the dear leader had been looking into

the matters related to the reception of foreign guests. Informed by an official concerned about the working conditions of the cameraman, he asked what transport the cameraman was going to use.

Knowing that he was to go up to Hamhung by car, the dear leader thought over the matter for a moment and then instructed that the best working conditions should be provided for the man who was to photograph the image of the great leader in diplomatic activities.

"You must see that the journalist of the Central News Agency takes the special train," the dear leader said. **"And let him return by air. I will contact the Civilian Airline."**

Thanks to his great solicitude the man could arrive in Hamhung in time.

The Hamhung citizens greeted the great leader with boundless enthusiasm and joy. Confetti of all colours was scattered over the streets, as the shouts of joy echoed round the place.

The fatherly leader, with a bright smile, acknowledged the enthusiastic cheers.

With an ardent desire to take the picture of this historic moment, a picture to convey the scene as it was, the cameraman repeatedly clicked his shutter.

When he arrived at the airport after his mission, the airplane sent by the dear leader was waiting for him.

It was four o'clock in the morning when he departed for his quarters in the outskirts of Pyongyang to prepare himself for the coming events after handing over the film bearing the image of the great leader.

He got off his car and walked quietly into the yard trying not to disturb other officials who were asleep.

On his way he met an official who hurried out at that early hour. The official warmly grasped his hand, asked why he was so late, and then told him what had happened last night. The dear leader had been waiting for him, ringing up three times.

Only a moment ago he called up the official asking if he was back yet and went on to say, "**You must see that the cameraman from the Central News Agency has a warm meal when he comes back from his mission. I'm afraid that he has not got his meals in time.**"

How tenderhearted and considerate!

Though he sat at the table spread with steaming rice and soup, the cameraman could hardly eat any food as he was overcome with surging emotions.

A New Building Sprang Up on the Potong River

One day several years ago the groundwork was prepared for a big building opposite the People's Palace of Culture across the Potong River, and a large number of building machines began to work on the basement and structural parts. This new building project drew the attention of passersby. The ground had been laid out and reserved for a monumental structure for a long time.

Who could have imagined that the new building rising magnificently on that ground was to be the one for the Central News Agency?

In July 1977, the dear leader Comrade Kim Jong Il was looking into the problem of the news agency office building and suggested to use the building under construction on the Potong River as such.

The exciting news reminded the news agency officials how the dear leader had been concerned about their office building all the time.

In November 1973, a leading official of the news agency was told by the dear leader to come to his office.

When he came the dear leader offered him a seat and said

that he had wanted to see him, but did not have time enough and that he had to put off all other work that day, in order to meet him.

The dear leader explained to him in detail about the important problems in news services.

After a long while he proceeded to the question of the office building. He said he was sorry that measures had not yet been taken to solve the problem of inadequate accommodation of the news agency building, though he had been aware of it. He added that they were probably having many difficulties at the news agency.

Their office building which was on the Taedong River at that time was good enough. Nevertheless, the dear leader was concerned over their office building. Indeed, he was always considerate enough to provide better conditions for the news agency. This was how the new building under construction on the Potong River was given to the news agency.

The news service people and the building workers strove to finish as soon as possible the construction project which was going on under the great care of the dear leader.

One afternoon when everyone on the whole construction site was working hard, an official came with a glad news. He said the dear leader had said that the building now under construction would be too small for the news agency and that, therefore, the second and third ones to be built should be turned over to them.

Everyone was stirred up with excitement, as the official went on saying that a few days before the dear leader called the official to his office and asked how things were going at the site.

The dear leader listened to the official's report for a while and then asked what was the floor space of the building now in use.

At the answer he got from the official, the dear leader was silent, probably comparing the sizes of the old and new buildings, and then remarked that new building No.1 would be too small for them and instructed that the two more buildings should be given to the news agency.

Informed of his further solicitude, the workers of the news agency were moved boundlessly.

After that the dear leader took measures to provide them with necessary equipment and materials, a reinforcement of builders and all other necessities to speed up the project. As a result, the new magnificent building was erected much earlier than expected.

On the memorable day, February 16, 1979, the news agency moved in the stately modern building thanks to the unremitting consideration of the dear leader, and from there they transmitted the first news.

The dear leader was more glad than anyone else at the fact that the news agency had started their work in the new building. Indeed, the new office building of the news agency on the Potong River is the symbol of the great love and care of the dear leader Comrade Kim Jong Il.

He Sent a Special Plane

In the spring of 1975 the great leader Comrade Kim Il Sung was visiting a socialist country on his historic foreign trip.

The people of that country warmly welcomed him. The whole land was in ecstasy.

In the excitement of being honoured with the mission of accompanying the great leader, a mission given by the dear leader who placed great political trust in them and showed them profound consideration, the cameramen transmitted by wireless the pictures of the enthusiastic welcome scenes to the homeland.

But at the homeland the pictures proved to be not very clear and therefore they requested for retransmission. They sent them again but the result was the same. They were at their wits' end, when an official hurried in. Gasping for breath, he warmly took the hand of one of the reporters and said in a quivering voice, "The dear leader has sent a special plane for you. Let's go to the airport with the films in a hurry."

Some time after a special plane carrying one or two reels of film left the airport for home.

It was like a dream, indeed.

Has there been such an instance in the history of the press?

There are cameramen in each country, but can any of them have the same honour of performing their duty under such tender care as shown to our cameramen?

This is the great love that can only be shown by the dear leader who regards it as his foremost and loyal duty to hold the great leader in high esteem, the supreme honour and happiness that can only be enjoyed by our cameramen who perform their honourable duty in his embrace. It is an eternal epic of tender care that should be conveyed to all succeeding generations.

Warmth of Care Reaches a Far-off Continent

In early May 1980 when the balmy spring was at its best in the mountains and fields, a special plane was flying over across the borders of our country and many other lands to the far-off Balkans.

Respected Comrade Kim Il Sung, the great leader of our Party and our people, was visiting a foreign country in order to take part in the funeral ceremony of the President of that country. Aboard the special plane was also a cameraman of the Party paper. He was feeling in his heart the exceptional trust the dear leader placed in him by giving him the honourable mission of accompanying the great leader.

The dear leader not only placed this great trust in him, an ordinary cameraman, but clearly explained to him the principles and direction of activity in that country.

Inspired with immense confidence and courage by his instructions, the cameraman firmly resolved to implement them to the letter.

There was one thing which was heavily weighing on his mind from the outset. He was picturing in his mind a large number of journalists from many countries crowding in the capital of that country, which would cause great difficulties in the wireless transmission of photos. Under these circumstances, sending in time the pictures of the respected leader in historic external activity to the homeland would pose a very serious problem.

The cameraman was haunted by the thought of how to overcome these predictable difficulties, but he could find no solution. This was a very heavy load on his mind.

In this mental state he began to record on films the beloved leader's activities in that country. When he had just finished his first shooting and closed his camera, a staff member of our embassy ran up to him, and urged him to go to his hotel, saying that the local people would come to install an exclusive line.

Dumbfounded at the unexpected words, he simply looked at the man's face.

"The dear leader has taken measures for an exclusive line," the man said, "so that the pictures of the respected leader's foreign activities can be sent home without delay."

At this moment of excitement he could not help

marvelling at the dear leader's superb organizational ability in taking measures well in advance.

As he knew it later, the dear leader had become deeply concerned over the photographic presentation of the external activities of the great leader on an unexpected trip to the funeral ceremony, because he had anticipated that the cameraman's wireless photo transmission would get stuck in the local conditions where the scene would be congested with journalists from all parts of the world. So he had taken an urgent measure to let our embassy in that country prepare an exclusive line for the cameraman.

When he arrived at his hotel in great excitement, there had already been installed a wireless photo transmitter on his desk.

The cameraman felt himself as if in a dream. Having produced the photos of the respected leader's activities, he sat at the desk, switched on the transmitter, and then called up Pyongyang.

Before 30 minutes passed, a clear and tender voice from the home station answered: "This is Pyongyang!" The cameraman felt the benevolent love of the dear leader in his heart and was unable to keep back the tears running down his cheeks.

Thus the first batch of photographs of the external activities of the respected leader was sent home.

He put all his energies into his work and sent home the photos of the respected leader's activities in that country without delay through the exclusive line provided by the dear leader.

Thus our people had the great happiness and joy of seeing in the Party paper the image of the beloved leader in his activities in that country.

THE SUN SHINES IN EVERY NOOK
AND CORNER OF LIFE

Concern about the Meals of Journalists

On August 10, 1963, the great leader Comrade Kim Il Sung and the dear leader Comrade Kim Jong Il were going to climb Mt. Paekdu during their on-the-spot guidance to Ryanggang Province, the historic place.

The journalists who were to accompany them, were deeply impressed upon hearing this happy news.

Mt. Paekdu is glorious with the immortal revolutionary history of the great leader who brought a new dawn of national liberation by creating the Juche idea.

It is the august mountain of revolution from which the dear leader rose as a bright lodestar in this country.

The vast forests of Mt. Paekdu were restless all night as the trees swayed, awaiting the new day of glory.

That night the journalists, too, could hardly fall asleep. Having hardly slept one wink, they got up before dawn and hastened with their preparations for the news coverage. They had nearly finished their preparations when one of their colleagues hurried to them and told them that the dear leader was strolling along the shores of Lake Samji.

When the journalists rushed out of the room, they stood glued to the spot. They saw the dear leader standing imposingly on the lakeside in a wet fog.

They knew too well that on the previous day, on the eve of the historic day when the great leader was to climb Mt. Paekdu, the dear leader was very busy making various arrangements and instructing them how to collect materials, till the late hours.

He was now gazing solemnly at Mt. Paekdu with its summit shrouded in mist.

As they were looking with respect at his noble figure, the journalists felt something solemn in their minds.

Just at this moment a rumbling voice echoed through the quiet shores of the lake: **"Comrade journalists, come here."** The dear leader was waving at them.

They hurried to him and courteously greeted him. As usual, with a broad smile, he asked them if they were prepared for the day's news coverage. They answered in the affirmative and added that they would climb Mt. Mudu ahead of anybody and make preparations to receive the great leader. He replied that they had better do so.

Hearing that they were going to set out at once, he asked in a solicitous voice if they had had their breakfast. They replied that they would take it after returning from Mt. Paekdu, because they would have to wait for some time until the meal would be ready. Their mind already flew to Mt. Paekdu with joy and emotion at the thought of ascending it accompanying the great leader and the dear leader.

Sensing their feelings the dear leader said with a kind smile:

"Today is a memorable day when the great leader will climb Mt. Paekdu. So you must make full preparations for collecting information.

"If you start right now, you may miss a meal. I can't allow you to start without having your breakfast. You have no time. So, you should go to the dining room and take that which is ready."

The journalists could say nothing for this parental love

of the dear leader, who was concerned about their meal, after he had conferred them a great honour.

At the moment a functionary who was near the journalists ran to the dining room to see whether the meal was ready. The workers of the dining room were puzzled not knowing what to do when they heard from him that the dear leader was concerned about the breakfast of the journalists who were starting to collect information early in the morning.

The rice and side dishes were ready but the soup was not yet prepared.

When he learned of this, the dear leader said with a bright smile: **"Never mind if the soup is not ready, but how could the journalists work without having breakfast?"** Then he addressed the journalists: **"You had better take what is prepared,"** and went ahead towards the dining room. The journalists could not follow him without a second thought. Having entered the dining room, they hesitated to move closer to the table in deep emotion.

Seeing this, the dear leader said: **"Comrade journalists, there is no need to stand on ceremony. Now, come nearer and sit down."** And he himself led them by the hand to seat them at the table. But they could not take spoons and chopsticks readily, feeling the boundlessly warm love of the dear leader.

The dear leader's great concern became the food of loyalty for the journalists. Thus that day they could creditably perform their honourable task to take a historic picture of the great leader who looked down the mountains and rivers of the country from Mt. Paekdu, the picture which was to be handed down to posterity.

To Give Them Even a Brief Rest

The dear leader Comrade Kim Jong Il takes utmost care of editors and other journalists naming them as heroes. He always worries himself about the journalists of the Party paper who work far into the night and pays special attention to lighten their burden.

In August 1973, the great leader Comrade Kim Il Sung gave on-the-spot guidance to Kangwon Province and the Tokchon district of South Pyongan Province.

At that time the great leader guided on the spot, for several days, the work of Kangwon Province and on the last day he attended an enlarged plenary meeting of the provincial Party committee far into the night. In spite of this, on the following morning he started for the Tokchon district.

The journalists of the Party paper failed to write an article on the enlarged plenary meeting of the Kangwon Provincial Party Committee in time because they had accompanied the great leader in his successive on-the-spot guidance. They barely managed to complete the draft of this article only on the night when they stopped to stay where the great leader was on the next leg of his guidance.

They regarded that the article should be examined by the great leader in view of its importance and presented the MS to him.

Feeling sorry for having presented the MS to the great leader so late at night, they were waiting impatiently for the article.

But they were informed that the great leader was so tired that he fell asleep on the chair, while reading the draft of the article at dead of night despite his fatigue from his long journey of guidance. They blamed themselves for their failure to write the article in time and also were greatly moved.

The dear leader must have felt sorry at seeing that the great leader had fallen asleep, the great leader who devoted his whole life for the people and was so much concerned for their happiness. The dear leader could not fall asleep that night, deeply concerned about the health of the great leader. And yet he was thinking of the editorial workers of the Party paper who would be waiting for the article to be published that day. He worried about their health and rest, for they had always worked till late at night.

He said that he would ask the great leader for permission to put off the editing of the article until the following day, and instructed that the editors should be given a good rest.

The dear leader's great love moved the journalists so much that they could not say anything. Though he never had a good sleep at night reading their articles while dealing with numerous important and difficult things, he thought first of the staff members who had to work through that particular single night.

The dear leader always takes loving care of the journalists and editors. He had snacks supplied to them at night due to his concern for their health and pays close attention to the smooth running of the Night Sanatorium for Journalists which was set up under the care of the great leader for their adequate rest.

Holding an Umbrella

On a rainy day early in August 1967, a young train announcer was connecting cut broadcasting lines with her associate at Sokhu Station in South Hamgyong Province.

At this moment someone was holding out an umbrella over her head. The announcer asked herself who this person could be.

She felt like finding out who it was and was attracted by his kindness. However, she had no time to do so. It was almost time for the train to leave, but she was much worried because she had not managed to connect the lines.

"The line is short. Supplement the line with the electric line in the passenger car. The passengers are waiting, so you should ensure timely broadcasting." A soft voice rang in her ear.

Her eyes were wide open and she was sure that in that way they would be able to connect the lines and ensure timely broadcasting.

"Who could be this man that is so well acquainted with our work?"

Only then did she look back and saw a man beaming with a bright smile. His dress was getting wet with rain drops streaming down from the umbrella. She was embarrassed.

However, he said with a generous smile:

"I don't mind my dress being wet. Don't worry about it. Can you now start broadcasting?"

"Yes, I can," she replied.

"All right, then. Try to do it well. I'll also listen to you," said the man, adjusting her armband. He read the words "train announcer" on the armband, which were embroidered in gold on a red background, saying:

"Train announcer is literally a real educator and a kind guide of passengers."

Listening to his remark the heart of the announcer was full of emotion. She thought to herself: "He must be a functionary in charge of broadcasting work."

He urged the girl, who was hesitating, to get on the train because it was the time for the train to start, and he held the umbrella open until she mounted on the steps lest she should be exposed to the rain.

Even when she held a broadcasting manuscript sitting in front of the microphone, her thoughts were fixed on the grateful man all the time.

"Who is he? The man with a bright face, sparkling eyes and a stentorian yet gentle voice?"

When she found out later on that the man was the dear leader, she was startled.

The dear leader Comrade Kim Jong Il!

How much she had been longing to see him!

Wrapped in solemn emotion, she ran out to the vestibule, but she could not see the dear leader.

Only then did she realize that the train was running.

At that very hour the dear leader was listening to train broadcasting, his dripping dress hung over the back of a chair at his compartment.

With the Feeling of a Father Desirous to Give One More

It was four o'clock in the morning of December 31, 1975.

Everybody in the capital was sleeping in peace. However, a bright light was beaming through the windows of the dear leader's office.

Having put all people to sleep in the cradle of happiness, he was reading the first proof of an editorial submitted by the *Rodong Sinmun*, at this early hour of the day.

He scrutinized every line, underlining and correcting sentences, words and phrases.

When he was through with the proof, he thought for a while.

Then he drew a list of the New Year gifts intended for the journalists and editors of the *Rodong Sinmun*.

It contained various kinds of foodstuffs and aromatic fruits that had been brought from faraway southern countries.

The dear leader read the list of gifts again and again as if he was not satisfied with them.

This morning he was very anxious to give at least one more thing to them, just as a father would do to his own children.

After a while, he summoned a functionary.

The functionary came to the dear leader's office in a hurry. Entering the room, he was vexed to look up to the dear leader who had worked all through the night. But the dear leader said he was sorry for calling him so early and went on: **"Comrades of the Party paper are taking too much trouble. Let's go to the storehouse and see if there is anything more we can give them."**

The functionary looked at the table where the proof of the editorial was lying, corrected by the dear leader in neat handwriting.

The functionary was deeply moved by the great fatherly love of the dear leader who, while reading an article, first thought of the troubles of the Party paper journalists who had written it and was always worried lest they should have a trivial inconvenience in their life.

The functionary wanted to tell the dear leader to have a rest even for a while and that he would arrange everything later, but he could not stop the dear leader who was already walking ahead of him.

The dear leader who had been looking round the storehouse accompanied by the functionary, made a sudden halt at one spot.

Instantly, his face brightened with joy, for he found deluxe fountain pens and ball pens in a corner; they were hardly noticeable.

It is said from olden times that a good article and a good handwriting depends on a writing pen. So the fountain pen and ball pen are always regarded as valuable things by the journalists.

Realizing the feelings of the writers, the dear leader told the functionary to give the journalists of the *Rodong Sinmun* these things in addition to the things which were already prepared. Then he walked with a happy mood, leaving behind footprints on the snowy way.

Looking up at the noble figure of the dear leader, the functionary said to himself: "Probably nobody in this wide world knows that there are journalists who live and work enjoying such a great love and under such meticulous care."

An Anecdote about the Dwellings of the Party Paper Journalists

In August 1975, Ragwon Street which was being newly built at the end of Potong Plain on the west of the capital on the occasion of the 30th anniversary of the founding of the Workers' Party of Korea (October 10), was nearing completion.

It was a very warm afternoon.

Despite such weather, the dear leader came out in this street lined with high modern apartment buildings. Giving instructions on the spot accompanied by the functionaries of the construction office, he dropped in Building No. 4, a 12-storied apartment.

He looked round the rooms with papered floors and walls and examined the nice furniture with great satisfaction.

After inspecting many rooms with different designs, he instructed the functionaries to make a shoe chest and a P.O. box for each flat, a problem which they had not yet given attention to. He also inquired in detail whether there was anything missing among the kitchen utensils, if rain water would collect in the balconies, etc.

Still feeling a weight on his heart, he left the place after asking them again and again to see that those who would move into new houses would have no inconveniences.

One autumn day several months later, the dear leader summoned a functionary and asked him in detail about the distribution of the apartment houses in Ragwon Street.

When he was informed for whom Building No. 4 was intended, the dear leader got up.

Building No. 4, which consisted of 60 flats, was the best of all the houses in this street in its location and structure.

Each flat had many living rooms provided with hot-water heating, various kinds of furniture, a TV set, a refrigerator, a washing machine and an electric pot. Near the house there were a kindergarten, a nursery, a school and various public service establishments and there were no traffic problems.

The dear leader who had been engrossed in deep thought about Building No. 4, expressed his desire to give the whole building to the editors and other journalists of the *Rodong Sinmun*. His unfathomable love for the newsmen made the functionary a happy man.

As a matter of fact, when distributing the houses of this street, the functionaries concerned also kept in their mind the journalists of the Party paper who worked hard at night. They had distributed much more flats to them than to workers of other organs.

Although he had been informed of this, the dear leader gave the whole building to the Party paper workers, a building which he had surveyed personally and considered the best one.

Until that day the functionary had regarded the dear leader's guidance to Building No. 4, given several months previously, as an ordinary one. Only now did he realize why the dear leader paid special attention to this building, during his guidance to the street, although he was extremely busy taking charge of all the affairs of the country.

When he understood his noble intention, the functionary could not raise his head with the sense of self-reproach. When they received the entrance certificates to the houses and moved in them, which had such a moving anecdote and were associated with the dear leader's warm love, the journalists and their family members felt proud at their fortune in being distinguished by the dear leader.

Wedding Banquet of an Editor

The dear leader Comrade Kim Jong Il embraces men of the press and looks after them with utmost care. His warm love is also expressed in the wedding banquet of an editor.

This happened on September 18, 1966. That day an editor of the Radio and TV Broadcasting Committee who had been working there for four years after serving in the People's Army, was going to wed.

From the morning his house was lively with preparations for the ceremony.

His colleagues and his relatives and friends did all they could in giving him assistance for his wedding.

All the preparations for the wedding had been made. Now the only thing to do was to hold the ceremony when the time would come. Just at this moment, a functionary came in with a big box in his hand. He said it was a gift from the dear leader Comrade Kim Jong Il.

All those present at the wedding, to say nothing of the bridegroom, were surprised and greatly moved.

Receiving the gift permeated with the love of the dear leader, with deep emotion, the bridegroom suddenly recollected the day when he had met him some time ago.

That day the dear leader was giving his on-the-spot guidance to the broadcasting committee. On the eve of his departure, he summoned the man. Already four years previously the dear leader had shown him great solicitude, meeting him at the music recording room and telling him: **"Let's make friends."**

That day when he met him again, the dear leader, smiling tenderly, asked quite unexpectedly about the date of his wedding. He had already been informed about his marriage. Blushing, the man gave him the date.

The dear leader parted, wishing him a good wedding ceremony.

And now, remembering the date of his marriage, the dear leader bestowed such a great favour on him.

The bridegroom took the lid off the box in humble reverence.

In the box there was the dear leader's autographed letter in which he congratulated the couple upon their marriage and wished them a happy married life. It also contained the wedding dresses for the bridegroom and bride, high-grade toilet articles and various kinds of rare food for the wedding banquet.

The bridegroom was greatly moved by the dear leader's warm love, a love which he hardly deserved.

When he thought of his wedding ceremony which was going on amid the blessing of the dear leader, it seemed to him that all the happiness of this world was intended for him and all joy of this world was meant for his own family.

Suddenly a horn of a car sounded. After a short while, a functionary rushed in and said that the dear leader was coming.

This was so unexpected that it seemed like a dream.

He could hardly restrain his gratefulness for the dear leader who had sent him, an ordinary editor, valuable gifts and a letter of congratulations on his wedding. And never did he dream that the dear leader would personally call at his house. In company with his bride he hurried out of the room.

The dear leader was already climbing up the stairway to the fourth floor.

Now he stepped towards the new couple, who were standing at a loss what to do, and said in a soft voice: **"Congratulations on your wedding day!"**

When he entered the room, the dear leader declined the cushion which was offered to him and sat on the floor unceremoniously.

Gazing affectionately at the new couple full of happiness, he said that they were really blessed and earnestly advised them never to forget the favours of the fatherly leader who had provided them with today's happiness.

Everyone looks back on his wedding day as a pleasant and happy day. But the couple were holding their wedding ceremony in the presence of the dear leader whom they had been so eager to meet even in their dreams. So they were delighted and happy beyond measure.

An amicable atmosphere and merry laughter prevailed in the room honoured by the presence of the dear leader. He congratulated the new couple, forming a happy family, under the benevolent care of the fatherly leader and advised them always to be faithful to him, thus making their life worthwhile.

He congratulated them again and gave valuable teachings which would serve as a guiding principle for the broadcasting workers in their work in the future, and went on: **"Our Party values the broadcasting workers. Therefore, you must be exemplary in work and life more than anybody else. The more the Party trusts and takes care of you functionaries, the more loyal you should be."**

That day he paid deep attention even to their family affairs after their marriage.

He arranged the wedding ceremony of a broadcasting worker, personally visited his house to show him warm love, and remained with them till late at night.

The editor and his bride came out of the room to see him off. The dear leader advised them in a gentle voice to form a harmonious and happy family with their concerted efforts and again wished them happiness.

It was an unusually bright and fine night.

Innumerable stars twinkling like gold jewels were brightly shining ahead of the dear leader.

An Entrance Certificate Permeated with His Affection

One day in September 1965, the dear leader Comrade Kim Jong Il phoned a functionary of the Radio and TV Broadcasting Committee.

The dear leader inquired of the functionary what he was doing and whether he was busy, before he asked him to come to his residence in the evening, saying that he would send a car.

When the functionary got to his residence, the dear leader received him gladly and told him to sit down.

The functionary put out and opened his memo, thinking that the dear leader would give him some task. But the dear leader gently put his hand on his shoulder and said to an official who was next to him: "**He has no parents, so I was going to arrange his wedding. However, some time ago I went to him and learned that he had done it all alone. I had given him my telephone number so that he could inform me if anything would happen. But he had done it secretly all by**

himself even without phoning me." With these words he burst into a broad laugh.

Then, gazing at the functionary who was dropping his head blushing, the dear leader said that he had done a good thing, though he had done it alone and asked in detail where his wife came from, what she was doing and if her parents were alive.

When he learned that she was also an orphan, the dear leader broke off with a cloudy expression for a while. Then he approached the functionary and said in a sympathetic tone: **"Well, you yourself have no parents, and now you say you have chosen an orphan for your wife. You say your wife was deprived of her parents when she was four years old. Then she must have had a hard time from early childhood."**

The dear leader who had been thinking something with a cloudy look awhile, now asked with a bright face where his residence was.

The functionary answered that he had not as yet got a house because he had not been married a long time. Then the dear leader asked again: **"Then, have you sent your wife to her native home again?"**

He replied that she had gone to her relative's home, to bid farewell to her mates, adding that she would come back soon.

The dear leader took out his memo and jotted down something, saying: **"You have married to live together, but since you have sent her back, she must be sorry."**

When the functionary said that he would get a house soon, the dear leader replied: **"I was sorry because you held your wedding alone. But now that I can help you, I feel somewhat relieved. I must get you a house, for I have failed to help you in your wedding ceremony."**

One day, after a little more than one month, the dear leader who was giving guidance to the broadcasting committee on the spot, summoned him again.

The functionary hurried to the dear leader, who greeted

him with a smile and, opening the door of his car, told him to get in.

The man hesitated not knowing what he meant, before he said that he would go on foot. Then the dear leader again asked him to get in the car. When the man got in, the dear leader sat him by his side.

When the car reached his hostel, the man said he would get off there. But the dear leader held him back by pressing his shoulder and then told him to accompany him.

Going through the central part of the city, the car was passing past the picturesque Potonggang Pleasure Park.

The man was watching the dear leader's looks not knowing what it all meant, when the latter stopped the car in front of a newly built modern apartment house in Potong Plain.

Getting off the car, the dear leader stepped towards the entrance of the building ahead of the broadcasting worker.

He went up the steps and stopped in front of flat No. 3 on the second floor and took a piece of paper out of his briefcase.

"Now, take it, it is the entrance certificate. I could not allow myself to give you an old house because yours is a new family. So I was somewhat late in trying to get you a new one. Go in and see whether you like it."

With these words the dear leader opened the door personally.

It was so unexpected that the broadcasting worker stood glued to the spot. He could not say anything and was only gazing at the entrance certificate in his hand.

He could not hold back his surging emotion. He was immensely happy enjoying the great love of the benevolent dear leader, a love which neither his parents nor his brothers could give.

GUIDING TO MAKE POLITICAL INTEGRITY IMMORTAL

"But They Have Still Twenty to Thirty Years to Write"

It was November 1, 1979, the 34th anniversary of the foundation of the *Rodong Sinmun*, the Party paper.

Late at night that day the dear leader met the Party paper reporters and its leading official.

With a bright smile, he praised the commentary and the articles about the unassuming heroes which had appeared recently in the paper. He said that he had called them in to give them an assignment for an important editorial for the Party paper.

He explained in detail all matters regarding the orientation and content of the editorial and the form of description.

Looking around the reporters he said: "This is the inauguration day of the *Rodong Sinmun*. Soon after founding our Party the great leader launched its newspaper. Thirty-four years has passed since then....

"We must well preserve the traditions of the Party paper established by the leader and carry them forward thoroughly. We must let the coming generations know well the role the *Rodong Sinmun* has played at each historical stage."

The dear leader was giving the Party paper workers an honourable mission to ensure that the cause of the Party

155

paper was carried forward by the younger generation.

The reporters themselves are masters who should carry forward the glorious traditions of the paper founded by the great leader and led by the dear leader.

When thinking of this, they felt a keen sense of honour and heavy responsibility.

Looking tenderly at the reporters for a while, the dear leader said that the veteran journalists were now growing old, including those present on that occasion.

At his words the veterans dropped their heads, feeling that they have not yet done much to prove themselves worthy of the expectations of the Party in spite of their old age.

The leading official stood up and said that some of them were near sixty.

Sympathizing with them, the dear leader said in a gentle voice, **"But they have still twenty to thirty years to write."**

These words expressed the boundlessly warm and tender care of the dear leader who was encouraging the reporters and would keep them under his wings of leadership to the end of their lives.

Those who were present at the interview were not quite carefree about their future.

When he said they had still twenty to thirty years to write, the dear leader knew these painful thoughts in their minds and meant to encourage them by giving them strength and trust. The reporters were deeply impressed with his profound words. After giving thought to the matter for a while, the dear leader went on:

"It is important for you to write, but you should now prepare to hand over your batons. It is also a revolutionary task to train your successors properly and hand over the batons to them. You should perform this task with honour."

The dear leader meant that the veteran reporters must shoulder the important task of having the glorious traditions of the Party paper established by the great leader carried forward and developed.

If it was to carry out its honourable mission, the Party paper must steadily train its reserve forces and radically improve their qualifications.

Thanks to the care and concern of the dear leader a large number of excellent university graduates were being assigned to the Party paper every year. Training them into reliable journalists for the Party was an important question in strengthening and developing the Party paper.

The dear leader entrusted this important duty to the veteran reporters, and this was one of the many instances in which he had expressed his great confidence in them.

His sincere words moved the reporters deeply, and they resolved to prove themselves worthy of his trust and expectation by working loyally and striving hard to make the newspaper a success.

Indeed, the warm love shown by the dear leader is a lasting factor that gives the reporters the strength of eternal youth.

To Keep Flowers in Bloom

One November day in 1982, the journalists and other workers of the Party paper were excited at the news that the dear leader Comrade Kim Jong Il had conferred a great honour upon a veteran reporter who was supposed to retire on a pension after his long service for the newspaper by appointing him to a new post on the editorial board.

All revolutionaries want to lead a worthwhile life to the end. But it is natural that they grow old till they can no longer carry out their revolutionary duties.

So they have to retire, relieved from their duty by the new

generation, lest they should be a burden to others.

This was the case with a newsman who had worked for the Party paper for a long time as head of a department. Being in his late sixties, he knew that his eyesight and memory were growing weaker and found himself incapable of coping with his duty. So he made up his mind to retire on a pension and officially brought the matter to the Party organization and the administrative authorities.

Informed of this fact the dear leader kindly saw to it that the newsman was reappointed to a suitable new job on the editorial board, instead of letting him retire.

The new job was a brain child of the dear leader, unprecedented in the history of our press. The new idea was prompted by his profound consideration.

With a good understanding of the place and role of the publications, radios and news services in the revolutionary struggle and construction work, the dear leader paid deep attention to the life and work and even the future problems of the reporters and editorial workers who are in direct charge of mass media. Thus he thought the idea of the new jobs on the editorial and commentary boards which would benefit the reporters and editorial workers now on the job who would soon grow too old to perform their present duties by providing them with the prospect of a worthwhile future for the rest of their lives. And some time ago a radical step was taken to institute these new jobs formally.

This is the expression of the great trust the dear leader places in the reporters and editorial workers as well as his immense expectation from them. He treasures them and takes care of them with such warm love that he ensures that they gloriously preserve their political integrity in revolutionary practice, writing, photographing and training the reserve forces to suit their physical conditions on the honourable posts entrusted to them by the Party even when they are beyond the ages of sixty and seventy.

Thus the dear leader has taken good care of the reporters and editorial workers even in their closing years, now showing boundless confidence and consideration for the retiring newsman by appointing him as the forerunner to the new post on the editorial board of the Party paper.

At this news all the reporters and workers of the Party paper were deeply moved by his boundless love.

Informed of his reappointment by the leading official of the newspaper, the newsman was enveloped in excitement at the infinite trust placed in him by the dear leader and at his warmest love.

The old journalist had received all the favours that a man can receive from the dear leader.

Looking back, it was the dear leader who had trained him into a journalist of the Party, it was he who suggested to confer the title of People's Journalist upon him for his small service performed as a nameless newsman of the Party paper.

This had been more than he deserved. But the dear leader again had accorded him the privilege of being a representative to the celebration of the 70th birthday anniversary of the great leader Comrade Kim Il Sung, the most honourable privilege which he could confer on him.

The dear leader's love and concern for him had been so great and exceptional that the journalist had never thought that he would be able to repay all these favours nor had he expected any more glory. Nevertheless, the dear leader reappointed him to the glorious post in which the man can preserve his political integrity gloriously even in his closing years.

Afterwards another veteran reporter of the newspaper was given the same favour, and the feelings of gratitude of all workers of the Party paper were beyond expression. The newsman who was well over sixty and was going to retire, was appointed as member of the commentary board so that he could go on working in the press circle with honour for the rest of his life thanks to the benevolence of the dear leader.

At the news the journalists of the Party paper were deeply moved by the profound affection and benevolence with which the dear leader got the new posts instituted for the veteran newsmen in addition to all the favours and confidence he had shown them when they were still young. They all firmly resolved to be loyal to the dear leader.

The Dinner Arranged in Honour of a Newsman of the Party Paper on His 60th Birthday

On October 6, 1982, a newsman who had long worked for the Party paper was surprised to find his 60th birthday dinner arranged by the dear leader.

By custom, such a banquet used to be given by the family of the man celebrating his sixty years.

Nowadays, however, people consider themselves still young at sixty and old enough to celebrate their old age only when they are ninety. So they feel awkward to follow the old custom. As a matter of fact, every one of our people enjoys a happy and long life, free from the worries of food, clothing and housing, and no one would feel sorry even if a dinner was not given on his 60th birthday.

The newsman, too, felt the same and did not care for the celebration of his 60th birthday which was drawing near, and he declined the offer of his families and relatives to celebrate the day.

He was surprised and excited when an official knocked at the door of his house carrying with him the food for the dinner to celebrate his 60th birthday, a gift from the dear leader.

His heart was full of emotions, happiness and gratitude as he and his family looked up to the portrait of the dear leader.

The favour shown him by the dear leader was so immeasurable that he did not know what to do, overwhelmed with joy, before he went in deep recollection.

Denied even the natural human rights in the old society, he had drifted here and there afar from taking the worthwhile road of revolution.

But the dear leader guided him to be loyal to the cause of revolution to the last and made his life more worthwhile in this world. The dear leader had shown him all favours whenever there was the smallest chance, sending gifts to him on national holidays, awarding him the honour of receiving the "Kim Il Sung Prize", the highest official commendation, and now arranging the dinner in celebration of his 60th birthday. Indeed, no words could describe the favours the dear leader had shown the journalist.

The journalist felt in his heart the depth of the dear leader's boundless love and care for the men and officials of the press.

His immeasurably warm and kindhearted love which was expressed on the occasion of the reporter's 60th birthday as well as in awarding him the prize for his service is the greatest honour for the political integrity of all reporters.

Lasting Creative Enthusiasm

The annals of the care with which the dear leader Comrade Kim Jong Il has guided and looked after the men of the press are replete with moving stories.

One of them gives an account of the dear leader giving vitality and youthful enthusiasm to a painter of the Kumsong Youth Publishing House who had been considered hopeless due to an incurable disease.

The painter became bedridden after 25 years of his service for the press.

Being aware of the nature of his disease he was determined to spend his remaining days in a worthwhile manner, though his days were numbered.

So he continued his work with great enthusiasm even on his sickbed.

His drawings attracted young readers. They often wrote to him for more interesting pictorials.

Whenever he received their earnest requests, he felt it more painful that he could not concentrate on his work. To alleviate the pain he bent all his efforts to drawing and teaching his son how to draw so that he would take his place at the publishing house.

On the night of September 15, 1978 when the painter, assisted by his wife and children, was working on the pictures for the children's newspaper, an unexpected news reached him that the dear leader had showered on him warm love and favours.

At the report that the painter had long been suffering from an incurable disease, the dear leader was deeply sorry and accorded him great benefits by ensuring that he was given treatment and paid as much as he was when on the job until complete recovery. The dear leader also got the desire of the painter and his son realized by having the son discharged from the People's Army to carry on with the job of his father.

The dear leader's warm care and kindness deeply moved not only the painter and his family but all the workers of the publishing house.

Illustrated stories are part of man's spiritual wealth, but nobody had ever considered them worthy of being a lasting heritage for posterity.

Such story books, while being passed from one child to another, had pages missing or torn. They were seldom reprinted, and their author has since been forgotten.

But the dear leader considered them a powerful ideological weapon for the education of the new generation, treasured them and warmly loved their authors.

The dear leader who sees the future of our country on the smiling faces of children, valued the picture tales which give laughter and ambition to the children and spoke highly of the painters.

With such a noble mind and kind heart the dear leader bestowed the great benefits on the painter who had been intent on his work, while suffering from his disease.

He is continuing his creative work with redoubled efforts while receiving medical treatment at a best-equipped hospital. His son, too, is doing work as a successor to his father.

A Reporter Saved Miraculously from the Jaws of Death

Here is a story of a man who was brought back to life under the dear leader's loving care after his 60 days' unconsciousness.

One day in April 1980, a reporter of the Kumsong Youth Publishing House was on his trip to Ryondupyong Senior Middle School, Pungso County, Ryanggang Province on the northern tip of our country. His mission was to cover a newspaper article about the laudable act of a class of graduates who had volunteered to work collectively at a socialist construction site. But he was trapped in an accident and seriously wounded.

He was in such a critical condition that his faint and spasmodic breathing was the only visible sign of life in him.

The question was if he were to die in his thirties, thus leaving a bright future behind him.

It was a pity, but he was in such a critical condition that local doctors in the Pungso area did not know from where to begin his treatment. The officials of the publishing house who hurried to the scene were dismayed.

How could they inform his mother, wife and little children of this sad news?

The more they thought, the more they got confused.

The dear leader came to know the fact before his family.

On the night of April 23, 1980, he got a detailed report of the critical case from an official of the Party Central Committee and ordered a helicopter immediately to the scene to take the patient to the Hospital of Pyongyang University of Medicine for the best treatment possible. He also saw to it that the Ministry of Public Health gave first aid to the patient on the way to the hospital.

The rescue operation went on all night, telephones ringing at the Ministry of Public Health, the medical university hospital, the air station as well as the local authorities in Pungso to carry out his instructions.

A helicopter was ready to take off, and an ambulance carrying competent doctors was running through the capital city.

The next morning the helicopter took off, carrying an official from the central authorities and doctors, and flew to Pungso to implement the instructions of the dear leader who was deeply concerned over the reporter.

The unconscious patient was picked up. In the plane the doctors gave necessary first aid, observing changes in the symptoms of the patient. The plane itself became a surgery. The pilot, too, worked with all the care to keep the patient undisturbed.

At this moment there came an order by wireless: "Do not take direct course over the ridge but continue level flight by taking a roundabout route. Take care not to disturb the patient.... Land at Hamhung and give him medical treatment. Give up the appointed landing point and land at Pyongyang Airport...."

The dear leader gave these directions in order to alleviate the sufferings of the patient. Thanks to his parental care the plane arrived at the destination in safety and the patient was sent to the rescue department of the medical university hospital where he was examined thoroughly by the doctors who had been waiting for him. They were from all the specialized departments such as the cranial nerve surgery, the limbs surgery, the internal medicine of circulation system, the thoracal surgery and the heart surgery. The result of this comprehensive examination showed that the case was almost hopeless.

The patient had been in a most critical condition because of body septicemia, cerebral concussion, bleeding inside the cerebral membrane, lungs hemorrhage, pelvic fracture, sore of the bruised tissues, etc.

According to documentary records and clinical experience, modern medical science has not yet proved successful in the treatment of such a critical case nor many doctors and clinical experts recognized the possibility of how the patient could be saved.

Under the circumstances the dear leader took further steps to ensure that competent medical workers and doctors from all parts of the country got together to discuss and work out the most rational and scientific methods of treatment.

Thus, a medical force of approximately 20 people including Doctors and Assistant Doctors got down to the task.

They held many consultations and decided to combine Western and Korean medicines and apply a new method of invigorating the patient and preventing incidental diseases.

Expensive Korean medicines were required in quantity. The dear leader saw to it that a medicine supply system was set up to provide promptly all the medicines necessary for the recovery of the patient.

The valuable medicines which were supplied under his loving care had remarkable effect on the heart and blood of the patient and gave life to innumerable cells of his whole body. Then an operation followed.

Inspired by the boundless love shown by the dear leader, members of the treatment group, reporters and editorial workers of the publishing house and even the outpatients offered their blood and flesh for the treatment of the patient. People in many parts of the country were also moved by the dear leader's profound concern for the patient and sent rare tonics and nutrients which they had kept for their own use, to the hospital expressing their wishes to see the patient recover as soon as possible.

After 60 days the patient's condition began to take a turn for the better. The dark shadow of death was now dispelled from the reporter. The hope of recovery brightened and the patient became conscious at last to the joy of everyone.

Satisfied and overjoyed at the news and wishing to show the bright smile of the reporter in good health to the whole country, the dear leader instructed that the happy news should be reported by the press media—newspapers, magazines, the TV and films. The reporter who had come back to consciousness after 60 days' coma and had been told about the happenings in the meantime, said:

"Great leader, dear leader, I thank you!"

In expressing the deep feelings of his gratitude, he spoke on behalf of the workers of his publishing house, and also on behalf of all the people throughout the country. These words were a song of gratitude and throb of a revitalized life.

The life which was saved from the jaws of death, was indeed a new life born of the great love of the dear leader.

This immortal life is walking stoutly in the worthwhile cause of the country in the sunshine of the great love.

Grief over the Death of Reporters

On a September day, 1974, a functionary hastened into the dear leader's office room. As usual the dear leader was busy handling the documents piled up on his desk. On seeing the official, he stopped working.

"Comrade dear leader," he said and hesitated. The dear leader sensed that something extraordinary had happened and asked what was the matter.

On the previous day, one of the editorial staff of the *Rodong Sinmun* was preparing the following day's issue. At that time the head of state of a foreign country was on his visit to our country, so the journalist had worked throughout the night and morning, handling the important news without going home to rest.

Around noon an urgent matter took him out of the office, where he went out by car.

But nobody knew that he was never to return. He was killed in an accident. Under pressure of work he had had no time to read a letter from his son who was in the army and he had left it still unopened in his drawer. His desk was covered by the papers which he had been working on.

This was so unexpected that all were dumbfounded.

The report of his death clouded the face of the dear leader with deep grief. "Has he left us for good? How could he do so?" the dear leader said to himself, hardly able to believe the brutal fact.

He walked up and down, unable to repress his grief over the loss of one of his beloved men.

He slowly walked to the window with the painful thought of the unbelievably sudden death of the man with whom he had talked at times on the phone and sometimes calling him to his office to give him instructions, only a few days before discussing about the day's issue of the *Rodong Sinmun*.

The dear leader stood silently for a while probably recollecting the image of the dead journalist of the Party paper, thinking of the grief of the editorial staff and all the newspapermen who had lost their revolutionary comrade, and the bereaved family.

With all these thoughts flooding in his mind, the dear leader quietly turned round from the window and said in a doleful voice:

"**Such a fine comrade is dead!... Such a fine comrade! He should be given an institutional funeral.**"

Still overwhelmed with grief, the dear leader repeated the name of the dead journalist.

With irresistible feelings of sympathy, he addressed the official who was going out of his room, and exhorted that the comrades of the Party Central Committee must attend the funeral. The funeral was held as instructed.

A week passed by. Having painful recollections even in the hours when he was under pressure of work, the dear leader, out of his deep concern for the bereaved family, saw to it that the bereaved sons were sent to the Mangyongdae Revolutionary School where the bereaved children of revolutionaries study and that his family received the same wages and treatment as they had done during his lifetime.

On April 14, 1978, four years later, the dear leader, while giving on-the-spot guidance to the *Rodong Sinmun* and inspecting the installations of the printing shop, recollected again the official who had worked hard to install printing machines.

The man was dead, but his political integrity was preserved for always under the warm care of the dear leader. Such an honour was not limited to this man only.

One night early in January 1978, a journalist of the

Publishing House of the Workers' Party of Korea suddenly died of an illness.

Informed of the death of this ordinary pressman the dear leader, out of deep sympathy, acquainted himself with his activity and even with his family situations.

Meanwhile, he stared for a long time at the politico-theoretical magazine *Kulloja* which was on his desk. Turning the pages of the magazine without saying a word as if recollecting his painstaking efforts, the dear leader said:

"As I was told, he was loyal to the Party and worked in good faith. I would like to send a wreath in my own name as well as necessary supplies for the occasion, and his children should be educated at a revolutionary school, and his family should be awarded the certificate of a socialist and patriotic martyr."

Looking at the wreath sent by the dear leader out of his deep sympathy for the death of the unknown journalist, all the journalists and editors were in tears of boundless happiness of working under the guidance of the brilliant leader and great teacher.

Awarding an Order to the Bereaved Child of a War Correspondent

In May 1968, with the 15th anniversary of victory in the great Fatherland Liberation War close at hand, ceremonies took place in all parts of the country to award state orders to the people who had performed distinguished service during the war.

Such a function was being held in the Chollima Hall of Culture in Pyongyang, the capital, amidst the great attention and excitement of the people.

From the outset, attention was focussed on a boy in

middle school uniform. He took a seat like a man among middle-aged and grey-haired war veterans.

Everyone watched him with curiosity.

The boy was the posthumous child of a war correspondent of the newspaper *Minju Choson* who fell on his mission at the foremost front during the war.

The boy had grown up in happiness in the blissful socialist society, learning from his mother that his father had fought well as a war correspondent till the last moment of his life.

That was all he knew of his father.

Under the parental care of the great leader the boy was as happy as any other children in the world. With the passing of time the craving for his father was gradually fading away from his mind. He was intent on his study.

The dear leader who is considerate with all our people did not forget this war correspondent and his distinguished service for victory in the Fatherland Liberation War, honoured his son by inviting him to the awarding ceremony so that the boy could know the service rendered by his father and carry on the cause left behind by his father.

When the boy was decorated with national flag order on his chest, all the participants rose up on their feet and warmly applauded, barely restraining their tears.

The young boy with national flag order on his chest and in an irresistible excitement shouted at the top of his voice: "Long live the great leader Marshal Kim Il Sung!" Tearful voices of excitement cheered in response. It was a surging emotion and a strong sense of honour and happiness of working for the revolution under the wise guidance of the great leader Comrade Kim Il Sung and the dear leader Comrade Kim Jong Il. It was a high sense of pride they took in leading an immortal revolutionary life under the care of the great leader and the dear leader.

www.ingramcontent.com/pod-product-compliance
Lightning Source LLC
Chambersburg PA
CBHW010741170426
43193CB00018BA/2913